112 MEDITATIONS

For Self Realization

Vigyan Bhairava Tantra

Translation and Commentary By
RANJIT CHAUDHRI

Updated Edition 2024

FiNGERPRINT!
An imprint of Prakash Books India Pvt. Ltd

113/A, Darya Ganj,
New Delhi-110 002
Email: info@prakashbooks.com/sales@prakashbooks.com

Fingerprint Publishing
@FingerprintP
@fingerprintpublishingbooks
www.fingerprintpublishing.com

ISBN: 978 81 7234 491 7

ACKNOWLEDGEMENTS

I would first like to thank God for giving me the inspiration, strength and wisdom to write this book.

There are a few wonderful individuals who have helped me with this book, who I wish to thank. Professor Udai Banerjee for his help with the original text, Mrs. Maina Bhagat and Gagan Das for their help in getting the book published, my wife Priya for her support and encouragement, Varez Dadina for her beautiful illustrations and Dr. Anjana Srivastava for her editing. At other times, I have also been helped by Mr. S. C. Mahtab, Bhawani Mahtab, Mona Puri and Sandeep Jalan.

To all of you, my heartfelt thanks and gratitude.

To Lord Shiva and Sharada Devi,
With love and gratitude.

CONTENTS

INTRODUCTION

The *Vigyan Bhairava Tantra* is one of the most important spiritual texts of the world. It is a text that shows you how to reach God. There are two important ancient texts on yoga that deal with the higher aspects of yoga- our search for enlightenment and happiness. There is the Yoga Sutras of Patanjali, where the sage Patanjali teaches yoga, and there is this text, the *Vigyan Bhairava Tantra*, where Lord Shiva teaches yoga. Although the text is mainly about enlightenment, what it has to say about happiness is truly remarkable, and has the potential to completely transform our life experience for the better.

The *Vigyan Bhairava Tantra* contains 112 meditation techniques for self realization. These are meditations given by Lord Shiva. They are meant for all of mankind. There are 112 techniques to cover all types of people, through all time. Some of these techniques are for people who lived in the past, and some are for those who will live in the future. These 112 meditations cover people of all kinds, keeping in mind their differing natures and temperament. You will find at least one technique here that is ideally suited for you. That technique will take you very quickly to God.

The *Vigyan Bhairava Tantra* is sometimes simply known as *Vigyan Bhairava*. Vigyan (pronounced Vig-yaan) means knowledge or understanding. Vigyan also means knowledge beyond the sense organs, or knowledge beyond our sensory perception. Bhairava is another name for Lord Shiva. Vigyan Bhairava means complete knowledge of God. It is a text that teaches us how to know and understand God fully. We can only know God fully when we reach God, or become one with God. *Vigyan Bhairava* gives 112 techniques through which one can unite with God.

The text is a dialogue between Lord Shiva and his consort, Parvati - between God and the Goddess. The Goddess is, in reality, not separate from God. She has taken on the form of being separate here, to help mankind. She asks God those questions that we, as individuals seeking enlightenment, would ask.

In the text, Lord Shiva gives 112 meditation techniques for enlightenment. Most meditation techniques practiced today are derived, in one form or another, from one of the meditations given in the *Vigyan Bhairava Tantra.* Most of the meditations are beautifully simple. They do not require an abundance of intelligence to understand or to practice them. But do not let their simplicity fool you. They open a door to eternity. They are like truth - simple, yet capable of unlocking the mysteries of life.

The *Vigyan Bhairava Tantra* belongs to a form of yoga and tantra called, Kashmir Shaivism. Kashmir Shaivism is a philosophy of non-dualism or monism. Most religions are dualistic. There is the individual and there is God. The individual is separate from God, and at the end of his or her life, is judged by God. Therefore in religions, we (the individuals) are separate from God and also distinct from each other. In the philosophy of non-dualism, we are not separate from God, and we are not separate from each other. There is only One, there is only God. There is no Reality but God. The fact that we look separate from each other is an illusion. Our sense organs do not show us the complete picture. Deep down, we are all connected. For example, we look separate from trees. A human being defines the boundary of his body by his skin. Similarly, we know where a tree begins and where it ends. A human being looks separate from a tree. However, humans breathe in oxygen and give out carbon dioxide. Trees do just the opposite. We are now beginning to understand that by destroying our forests, and our environment, we are in fact destroying ourselves. We cannot survive on our planet, if there are no trees. Yoga and tantra understood this centuries ago. They teach that all forms of life are deeply connected. We are all part of God. There is no Reality apart from God.

The *Vigyan Bhairava Tantra* contains a great deal of practical wisdom. Its message is meant to be applied in our day-to-day lives. It shows us directly how to bring peace and joy into our lives. Although it was taught over 4000 years ago, its message is eternal. It was meant for all times.

The dialogue begins with the Goddess asking God about the true nature of God. The answer comes surprisingly quickly, in Verse 15 itself. Verse 15 explains to us that we can experience the joy of God within ourselves, when the mind is still and free of thoughts. In other words, we achieve liberation, when we still the mind. This text, and Kashmir Shaivism, state that union with God is not a meeting of two; it is a meeting of one. When the mind is stilled, our ego disappears and the state of God appears within us. Liberation is nothing but the awareness of our true nature.

The book has great practical value because it addresses an issue fundamental to most of us – our search for happiness. Lord Shiva shows us that we are looking for happiness at the wrong place. We will find permanent happiness within and not in the exterior world. The bliss we experience within is far greater than anything the external world can offer. The external world is subject to change, and the cycle of pleasure and pain will continue. We cannot have one without the other. Nor is it possible to completely control the external conditions of our lives. We solve one problem and another one arises. The way to peace and happiness is not to seek perfection in our external life situation (which is impossible), but to control our mind so that external conditions do not bother us. No situation or problem causes us suffering. It is our thought about it that causes us pain. Remove the thought, and we are at peace. The greater control we have over our minds, the more peace and joy we experience. When the mind is completely stilled, we experience bliss.

Whether we are seeking enlightenment or happiness, the key here is to control the mind. For this, 112 meditations have been given.

The meditations given in the text begin slowly. The first few meditations are primarily sitting meditations, to be practiced seated, with eyes closed. Then suddenly, from Verse 43, the text shifts gears and moves to an entirely different level. It introduces us to the concept that our beliefs create our reality. By changing some of our beliefs, we can liberate ourselves. There are many meditations given in this text that follow the same principle. The principle that our beliefs create our reality has many wonderful practical applications. We can change the external circumstances of our lives, by changing some of the beliefs that caused them.

There are some meditations given in the text that change our perception of life. They change the way we perceive or look at things. This process awakens us to a higher reality and changes our behavior immediately. For example, Verses 100, 107 and 124 explain to us that the same God that is present in oneself, is present in everyone else too. This means that no one is special. It does not matter how wealthy, intelligent, accomplished or evolved we are. None of these things makes us superior or inferior to anyone else. When we understand this truth, we become more humble, and our behavior towards everyone else changes automatically.

There are many other beautiful meditations given in the text that have the ability of awakening us from our dream state, and propelling us to a higher reality.

After the meditations, the dialogue between God and the Goddess continues, and certain aspects of the philosophy of non-dualism are discussed. At the end of the book, one final meditation is given. This meditation is special. Even when all other meditations fail, this one always succeeds. It is easy to practice and works for everyone.

The question sometimes arises as to whether the *Vigyan Bhairava Tantra* is a text on tantra or yoga. Actually it is both. It is primarily a text on yoga. However, yoga was initially part of tantra. Therefore, it is also a text on tantra. Tantra also includes many other rituals and practices that have nothing to do with yoga. Today, people harbor the misconception that tantra is about sex. That is incorrect. Tantra is mainly about enlightenment. There are only 3 meditations out of 112 given in this text that use sex as a means for enlightenment.

I have relied mainly on the original Sanskrit text given in the Kashmir Series of Texts and Studies, for my translation. The original text is continuous, but here it has been divided into three parts. The first chapter deals with the initial questions and answers between God and the Goddess. The second chapter contains the 112 meditations given by God. The third chapter contains the final questions and answers between God and the Goddess.

Kashmir Shaivism is at least 5000 years old. Lord Shiva first taught yoga to the seven sages, the *Saptarishis*, about 10,000 years ago, at Mount Kailash, in present day Tibet. He gave them 112 methods for liberation. Are the 112 meditations contained in this text, the same as the 112 meditations given by Lord Shiva to the seven sages? They probably are, although we cannot be sure. Two of the sages returned to India and imparted the teachings of yoga in this country: Agastya and Kashapa. Agastya taught in South India and Kashapa in North India. Rishi Kashapa is the founder of Kashmir and Kashmir is named after him.

Kashmir Shaivism flourished in the region of Kashmir for a few thousand years, till the 14th century AD, when Kashmir came under Islamic rule. The following centuries were tumultuous, with periods of repression and forcible conversions. Kashmir Shaivism survived the turmoil and continued to flourish outside Kashmir.

Kashmir Shaivism has a strong element of Devi worship, worship of the Goddess. Sharada Devi was the most popular Goddess worshipped in Kashmir. The main Sharada Devi temple, Sharada Peeth, was at one time not just a temple but also a flourishing university that attracted students from all over India. Sharda Peeth is currently located in Pakistan occupied Kashmir and is in a state of ruin.

There is one area India has always excelled at. Other nations may have produced more Nobel prize winners or Olympic medal winners but India has produced the maximum number of enlightened human beings. We have had a Rama, Krishna, Buddha, Mahavira, Patanjali, Guru Nanak, Kabir, Swami Vivekananda, Ramana Maharshi, Mahatma Gandhi and countless others. The reason for this is simple. The tools and technologies for enlightenment were first developed here. It all started with the 112 meditations given by Lord Shiva to the seven sages. The science of inner transformation and liberation was developed and preserved in this country. That is the true wealth of this nation. Some of that knowledge is contained in this text.

CHAPTER 1

THE QUESTIONS

From the unreal lead me to the Real.
From darkness lead me to Light.
From death lead me to Immortality.

—Brihad-aranyaka Upanishad

The first thing to understand about the *Vigyan Bhairava Tantra* is that it is a story of love. It is a dialogue between Shiva and Parvati, the God and the Goddess, who are deeply in love. The emphasis on love is significant. It is meant to convey several important truths. It is through love that we can understand God and know Him. To reach God, we must love, and love unconditionally. As Krishna said in the *Bhagavad Gita*:

O Arjuna, only through undivided devotion, is it possible to know, to see and to attain my true state, and to experience Me in such a form. (11.54)

The emphasis on love is found in other spiritual traditions. Buddha taught in the *Dhammapada*, that any supposed truth that could not be spoken in love, was not truth. That is why all great tantric texts were written in a language of love – as a dialogue between the God and the Goddess.

Love between a master and a disciple is also important. The Goddess is here taking on the role of a disciple, to help all of mankind. When a disciple is learning something new, it is important for the disciple to temporarily set aside what he or she thinks she knows about God. This will enable her to receive her master's knowledge.

When the disciple loves her master, she is willing to accept her master's wisdom, no matter how radically different her master's wisdom is from her own. With love, there is a trust, a faith in your master. Consequently, one is willing to try something new that can help one reach God.

Finally, love is important because in love, dualism is transcended. A sense of oneness is felt. Two persons who are deeply in love, sometimes lose their sense of individual identity. When a person loves deeply, she leaves her ego, or her individual identity behind. To reach God, one has to transcend one's individual identity. This happens automatically with love.

The Goddess said:

☙ 1 ❧

I have heard everything originating from the union of God and the Goddess. From the essence of the Trika System, along with its subdivisions. But, O God, even now my doubts have not been removed.

The Goddess is referring to texts of tantra dealing with liberation, including one called the *Rudrayamala Tantra*. (*I have heard everything originating from the union of God and the Goddess.*) Rudrayamala literally means union of God with his opposite (the Goddess). The *Vigyan Bhairava* was originally part of the *Rudrayamala Tantra*. The *Rudrayamala Tantra* is a text that has mostly been lost. The Trika System refers to the philosophy of Kashmir Shaivism. The Goddess has heard everything in the texts of tantra but still her doubts have not been cleared.

☙ 2 ❧

O God, what is your real nature? Is it a collection of words?

This is the first question the Devi or the Goddess, asks God – *what is your real nature?* Without waiting for a reply, the Goddess gives her own answer. Her answer is from some of the other texts of Kashmir Shaivism. It is important to understand that the Goddess is not separate from God. She has taken on a separate form here, to help genuine seekers of the Truth. She is asking those questions that all students of yoga and tantra would ask, even those who have read all the required scriptures.

Is it a collection of words? This refers to the Theory of the Alphabet. The theory explains how from the sound of the alphabets, the various constitutive elements of the universe are formed.

☙ 3 ❧

Or does the nature of God consist of nine different forms? Or is it a combination of three different heads, or three energies?

Three energies refers to the three energies of God – Supreme energy, medium energy and inferior energy. Energy is the creative aspect of God. It is through Energy that God creates the universe and all forms in it. In tantra, the Goddess is Energy. The word *shakti* used in Sanskrit, is translated sometimes as

Energy and sometimes as the Goddess. The words Energy and Goddess are frequently used interchangeably. Supreme Energy is when the God and the Goddess are one. There is no distinction between the two. Medium energy is energy that is used as means for the individual to return to God. Inferior or lower energy refers to the individual and all the individual forms of the universe. The three energies are more commonly known as God, Goddess and individual, or Consciousness, Energy and matter. It is important to understand all of it is one Energy. This one Energy takes on different forms or characteristics. In its highest form, it is known as Supreme Energy. When it takes on the form of an individual or an object, it is lower energy. But it is all one Energy displaying its different aspects.

☙ 4 ❧

Or are you consisting of sound, or point, or half moon? Is your nature that of energy ascending the chakras, or is it the voweless sound?

Sound refers to the sound of the alphabets that are the building blocks of the universe. *Point* is a reference to the light that is present in all objects. Some spiritual traditions believe that all created matter comes from sound and light. *Half moon* refers to energy that appears in a curved form. *energy ascending the chakras* and *voweless sound* is a reference to meditation techniques used to reach God.

5

Is medium and inferior energy divisible in parts? If that is also the nature of supreme (transcendent) energy, then it is inconsistent with transcendence.

6

The Supreme Being is certainly not a division of color or bodies. How can the Supreme Being be indivisible and yet be a composite of parts? O Lord, be gracious on me, and remove my doubts completely.

In these two verses, the Goddess is getting to the core belief of tantra – the philosophy of non-dualism. *Is medium and inferior energy divisible in parts?* The Goddess is asking whether individual life forms (inferior energy) are separate from each other. Are they divisible? Are they distinct or separate from each other? We certainly *look* separate and distinct from each other. If the answer is yes, we are separate from each other, then how can you say that God is within us? That in essence we are only God (Supreme Energy)? God cannot be divided into separate parts, into different colors or bodies. God is the Whole, indivisible. Therefore, how do you reconcile these two opposing truths. On the one hand, tantra says we (individual forms) are all part of God, or are all filled with God. Yet each form or life form is separate from each other (it appears that way). And God cannot be divided into separate forms or parts.

How can the Supreme Being be indivisible and yet be a composite of parts? Therefore, the Goddess is implying that if individual forms are separate from each other, you cannot say that we are composed of God, because God cannot be divided. These individual forms must be composed of something else. Are we therefore separate from God and separate from each other? The Goddess has basically presented the argument of dualistic traditions. These traditions or religions teach that we are separate from God, and distinct from each other. To put it simply, the Goddess is asking that, as God is indivisible, how can individual forms be separate and yet be a part of God.

God said:

7

Excellent! Excellent! Dear one, you have asked the essence of tantra.

The Goddess has asked two questions: What is your real nature (Verse 2), and how can individual forms be part of God when they are separate (divisible), because God is indivisible.

8

Dear one, even though the subject is very difficult to understand, I will explain it to you. Whatever has been declared as the divisible forms of God –

☙ 9 ❧

Know that O Goddess to be insubstantial, like a magic show, or like an illusory dream, or as an imaginary city in the sky.

What God is saying here, is that what you are seeing is not real. It is an illusion. *Whatever has been declared as the divisible forms of God – know that O Goddess to be insubstantial, like a magic show, or like an illusory dream.* The key words here are *divisible forms.* The divisible forms are an illusion. They are not real. We are not separate from God and from each other. For example: While watching a movie we see images of separate human beings and other life forms on a screen. These images are not real. They are just images. In actual fact, there is only a screen, and a projector, creating those images on the screen. The world is something like that. Images on the screen of God, where God is all three, the projector, the screen and the images on it.

Two questions now arise. If this world is an illusion or dream, then what is its purpose? Tantra says that the world is God's play. However, the world is important. It is necessary, so that God can experience his own nature. A contrasting field is necessary to experience the Ultimate Reality. Without "large", we would not be able to experience "small". Similarly, without "pain", we would not know "pleasure". If there is a place in this world where everybody is large, nobody is actually large because they do not know what small is.

Essentially, no definition or description can exist without its opposite. It cannot exist in a vacuum. A person cannot be "good" unless you know what "bad" is. Yoga says God's essential nature is joy. For God to experience his own joy, the relative world is necessary. Without the world of opposites, God would not be able to experience his/her nature. There would only be void, *shunya.* This is the difference between the Hindu and Buddhist concept of God. Hindus say God is Joy and Consciousness. Buddhists say the Ultimate Reality is Void. They are both correct. They are two sides of the same coin. God is Joy and Consciousness, but without the relative world, the illusion, God is Void.

Interestingly, this text uses a number of words for God. Shiva, Deva, Bhairava, Supreme Reality, Supreme Space, Supreme, Brahman, and yes, also Void.

This theory would also explain why the concept of heaven and hell, as expounded by some religions, would never work. If a person was in hell experiencing never-ending pain, after a while pain would not be pain, it would be nothing. If one continuously experiences pain and nothing else, then after a while pain would lose its meaning. In order to experience pain, one also has to experience its opposite, pleasure. Without its opposite, pain is no longer pain. It becomes nothing. For the same reason, heaven would never work. If you continuously experience pleasure without experiencing any pain, then after a while the experience of pleasure becomes nothing.

The second question that arises is that if the world is an illusion, how can we experience or know the Real? The answer to that is given in Verse 15. The sages of India were always concerned with finding the truth behind the illusion -

separating the Real from the unreal. There is a beautiful prayer in the *Brihad-aranyaka Upanishad* on this search for truth. As far as spiritual poetry goes, there is very little to surpass its beauty:

From the unreal lead me to the Real.
From darkness lead me to Light.
From death lead me to Immortality.

ൽ 10 ൾ

These concepts are used as a support for meditation for people of confused minds, who are interested in performing external actions. It is only for those people who are stuck in dualizing thoughts.

God now addresses the concepts put forth earlier by the Goddess. As to whether God consists of nine different forms, sound, point, etc. are for people *stuck in dualizing thoughts.* For those people who see themselves as separate from God and who cannot reconcile to the idea of God and themselves being One. Such people are more interested in performing rituals and external actions, than in meditating or going within.

ൽ 11 ൾ

In reality, God is neither of nine different forms nor a collection of words. Not of three heads and nor of three energies.

☙ 12 ❧

Not sound or point, nor half moon.
Ascending the chakras is not my essence,
and nor is energy my nature.

God is now beginning to address the Goddess's first question – *what is your real nature?* In these two verses, the suggestions made by the Goddess are refuted. The real nature of God is not what the Goddess has suggested. *Not sound or point, nor half moon.*

The Goddess can now well ask that if all these concepts are not God's nature, then why have all these concepts been mentioned in some tantric texts, as being God's essence. The reply is given in the next verse.

☙ 13 ❧

These concepts are for those whose intellect is not mature enough to understand Ultimate Reality. They are just like a mother who frightens children away from danger, and encourages everyone to commence their spiritual practices.

Some people are not able to understand God's true nature. The concepts of God's nature as suggested by the Goddess are meant for such people. They help these people, who are unable to grasp Ultimate Reality, to start their spiritual journey. These concepts lead one towards God. Once these people start their spiritual practices, their understanding of God increases. These concepts are then no longer required, and can be discarded.

☙ 14 ❧

I am free of all concepts of time or direction. I am not at a particular place. It is impossible to accurately represent or describe God in words.

Before explaining what God's real nature is, God is first explaining what it is *not.* The past few verses have stated that God's nature is not what the Goddess has suggested. This verse continues on the theme of what God is not.

God cannot be described in terms of time or direction. God is beyond all concepts of time or direction. *I am not at a particular place.* God is not some superior being, residing at a particular place. God is everywhere, filling everything completely. This verse is saying that it is not possible to limit God. To confine God to a particular place or time. *It is impossible to accurately represent or describe God in words.* Words in any language would not be able to accurately describe God. This is because words and descriptions belong to the mind. To know God, we have to go beyond the mind. To know God, we have to experience God. Words are only a poor substitute. It is for this reason that the words and teachings of masters who have experienced God, are easily misunderstood. Their words attempt to describe experiences that cannot be described in words.

☙ 15 ❧

One may experience the joy of God within oneself, when the mind is still and free of thoughts. That state of God full of bliss, is the Goddess.

Verse 15 is one of the most important verses in the entire text. It explains the basic philosophy of yoga and tantra. In the past few verses, God has explained God's nature in a negative manner – in terms of what God is not. In this and the next verse, God's nature is being explained in a positive manner – by describing what God is.

One may experience the joy of God within oneself. God's nature is joy. The key word here is *within*. We can experience the joy of God within ourselves. Human beings are similar to the Musk deer. The male Musk deer emits the musk scent from a pouch located in it. It searches frantically all over for the source of the scent. Sometimes, this search leads it to slip and fall over mountain cliffs, to its death. If only the deer had looked within, it would have found what it had been looking for – the source of the scent. Human beings are like that. We search frantically for happiness in the external world instead of within. We strive endlessly for fame, fortune and security, falsely believing that they will bring us eternal happiness. Achievement has also now become very important for us. Many people believe that unless they achieve something material in their lives (usually quantifiable in money), they will not be happy.

The greatest joy we can experience is the joy of union with God. In this verse, God is teaching us that this joy can be experienced within oneself. It is millions of times more than any joy we can experience in the external world. It is pure bliss and ecstasy. Any individual who experiences this joy for even a fraction of a second, would not give it up for anything in the world. Not for money, fame or anything else.

A very important spiritual truth is being stated here. We need nothing external to ourselves to be joyful. We don't need money, jobs, security, fame, or the approval of other people to be happy. We are truly individuals without need. The greatest joy we can experience, we experience within. Once experienced, nothing in the external world matches it. People who understand this truth, find their lives changing dramatically. They stop competing with others and start sharing more. Material achievements cease to be their primary concern. Instead, they focus their attention on seeking the true source of joy within. They work more productively without stress, and their lives become more joyful.

When the mind is still and free of thoughts. This is the key. The key that unlocks the door to eternity. To experience the bliss of union with God, one has to still the mind. Under normal circumstances, we are not able to control our thoughts. Our mind jumps from one thought to another. To know God and to unite with God, one has to control the mind. The mind is like a layer of dirt on a mirror. When there is dirt on a mirror, we are not able to see ourselves. When the dirt is removed, we are able to see ourselves clearly. Similarly, when the mind is stilled, we see our True Self. Verse 9 mentioned that our world is an illusion. We see the True Reality beyond the illusion, when we still the mind.

Yoga is not interested in improving or sharpening the mind. Rather, it is interested in transcending the mind. When we gain control of the mind, then we are no longer subject to its whims and fancies. If we want to think, we think. If we don't want to think, we don't. People who are not in control of their minds are not able to do that. They cannot stop the flow of thoughts. Try it out yourself now. Try to stop thinking for five minutes - not to allow a single thought to enter, for five minutes. If you succeed, you will be fully enlightened.

Awareness is required to reach God. When we think, we cannot be aware. Thinking and awareness do not go together. That is why all spiritual traditions emphasize stilling the mind. Buddha used to teach that conquering one's own self is better than conquering the whole world. Yoga says the same thing in a different way. Yoga teaches that it is better to change oneself, than to change the world. If this simple advice was followed by everyone, most of the violence and terrorism prevailing in the world today, would end.

The mind is an essential part of our ego. When our mind is stilled, our ego disappears. We become pure Awareness. In Kashmir Shaivism, union with God is not a meeting of two. When we achieve liberation, we do not meet God, embrace God and then unite with God. It is a meeting of One. When the ego *disappears,* God *appears.* When the ego appears, God disappears. Abhinavagupta, the greatest of the Kashmir Masters, used to teach that liberation (*moksha*), was nothing but the awareness of one's true nature. Our true nature is something that is *uncovered.* God is within all of us. God needs to be *uncovered.* We realize this when our mind is stilled or our ego is dissolved. "Is it not written in your law, I said, Ye are Gods?" (Bible, John 10:34)

Lord Shiva lays down the key requirement for liberation in this verse – stilling the mind. He does not go into any further detail after this. He instead expounds on techniques that can be used for achieving this objective.

That state of God full of bliss, is the Goddess. There is no difference between the God and the Goddess. This is a point that is explained in the following verses.

☙ 16 ❧

One should know my essential nature to be that joy, pure, and pervading the entire universe. As this is the nature of the Supreme Reality, who is to be worshipped and who is to be satisfied?

In yoga and tantra, the essential nature of God is joy (or love), and consciousness. Joy is mentioned in this verse, consciousness is mentioned later in the text. The joy of God pervades the entire universe. The universe is nothing but a part of God. Thus, the joy of God pervades the universe and everything in it. Our essential nature is also joy. We are not born in sin, as some religions claim. We are born in joy. Joy is not just our birthright. Joy or bliss is who we are. As the Taittiriya Upanishad beautifully states:

> *He realized that God is bliss. It is in fact from bliss that all beings are born. Once born, they live by bliss and when they depart, they merge into bliss.*

If our essential nature is joy, why is it that we don't always feel joyful? Why are our lives sometimes filled with tension, pain, suffering, fear and sadness. The answer is given in the previous verse. We suffer because of the non-stop chatter of the mind. When our mind is stilled, we experience the joy of our true nature.

There are moments in life when the mind suddenly stops working. It does not have to only happen when you are meditating. It can happen when you are walking alone, or driving a car. You experience a surge of joy spreading all over you. You can't stop smiling. External events no longer have any effect on you. Someone cutting you off in traffic, or being rude to you, has no impact on you. You feel incredibly light and happy. It is a wonderful experience! Even if a person experiences this joy for a brief moment, he/she longs to recapture this feeling.

As this is the nature of the Supreme Reality, who is to be worshipped and who is to be satisfied? In Ultimate Reality there is only One, there is only God. God pervades and fills the entire universe. There is nothing apart from God. Therefore, who is there to worship? Who is there to satisfy or please with our worship? The worshipper and the worshipped are not separate from each other. They are one and the same.

God needs nothing. God is everything and has everything. When there is only God, why would God need anything? Some religions talk of an angry God who demands things/certain behavior from us. If we fail to meet God's demands or expectations, we will be punished for all eternity, it is believed. However, the God of yoga and tantra is a God of joy. A God who is content in its own joy, and needs or demands nothing.

☙ 17 ❧

In this way, God's highest state is celebrated. Through that highest form of mine, the highest form of the Supreme Goddess is also being celebrated.

There is no difference between the God and the Goddess. In yoga, God is said to be joy and consciousness. Energy (*shakti*), the creative aspect of God, is the Goddess. The differentiation is made to help one understand the different aspects of God. In Ultimate Reality, there is no difference between God and Goddess. God and Goddess are also part of dualism. There is only one Supreme Reality that is neither male nor female. It is for this reason that the *Vigyan Bhairava Tantra* sometimes refers to God as Supreme Reality, Supreme, and Supreme Space. It is for the same reason that sculptures and pictures of Lord Shiva sometimes depict Him as *Ardhanariswara*, half male, half female. In these sculptures, half of the body of Shiva is shown as male and half as female. This is done to show that God is neither male nor female.

☙ 18 ❧

No difference ever exists between energy and the possessor of energy, between duty and being dutiful. For this reason, there is no difference between Supreme Energy (Goddess) and God.

Some of the dualistic philosophies of India show God's energy as being separate from God. In these philosophies, the created world, which is nothing but God's energy, is seen as separate from God. Verses 18 and 19 refute these dualistic philosophies.

There is no difference between Energy (Goddess) and the possessor of Energy (God). Therefore, there is no difference between Goddess and God.

꧁ 19 ꧂

The burning power of fire cannot be considered separate from fire. It is only described separately in the beginning, to enable one to learn its essential nature.

The Goddess is Energy. She is the creative aspect of God. Through Energy the entire universe is created. Energy is in all matter. Matter is nothing but energy vibrating at a certain frequency. Yoga and tantra have been saying this for centuries. It is only recently that science is beginning to accept this truth – that all matter is created by energy.

The burning power of fire cannot be considered separate from fire. Therefore the creative aspect of God (the Goddess), cannot be considered as separate from God. It is described separately, so that one can learn the different aspects of God. For this reason, the entire universe and everything in it (which is nothing but energy), is not separate from God. It is all a part of God.

☙ 20 ❧

When one has entered the state of Divine Energy, one is in the state of God. For it is stated here that the Goddess is the entrance to God.

☙ 21 ❧

Just as, by the light of a lamp and the rays of the sun, portions of space, etc., are perceived. Similarly, O Dear One, through the Goddess (Energy), God is known.

These two verses state that God is known through Energy (Goddess). There are two things implied here. Firstly, each person has dormant energy called *Kundalini* located near the end of the spine, at *Mooladhara Chakra*. Kundalini and the chakras are discussed in greater detail later on. Some of the meditation techniques attempt to raise this dormant energy through the spine, to the top of the head. When this event occurs, we are said to be in the state of Divine Energy mentioned in Verse 20. This state is also the state of God. This means that in this state there is full awareness and total joy. When we raise this energy of life up our spine, we find awareness and joy increasing. Therefore, through the Goddess (Energy), we reach God (Awareness and Joy). These concepts are discussed in greater detail in the meditations.

Verse 21 also states that through the Goddess (Energy), God is known. There is a more important meaning here, not just the one given in the preceding paragraph. When God's energy is dormant, God is inert. It is through Energy, the creative aspect of God, that God's nature is known. The example of a lamp is given. If a lamp is unlit, then one would not be able to see anything. Once the lamp is lit, then one can see the lamp and other objects in the room, and examine their nature. God is similar to the lamp and everything else in the room. The light of a lamp is like God's energy. When the light of the lamp is on, then the nature of the lamp and every object in the room, can be known. In the same way, only when God's energy is active, can God's nature be known. It is through God's energy (the Goddess) that God is known. The entire world is Energy. It is through the world that God's true nature is known. This is a concept that was explained in Verse 9. The relative world is necessary in order to experience Supreme Reality. In the absence of darkness, light could not be experienced. Similarly, to experience the joy of God, we have to experience something that is not joy. If we continuously have one experience without its opposite, then that experience would lose its meaning. If we continuously won in every situation in life, the feeling of winning would become meaningless. We need the experience of losing to give value to the experience of winning. Similarly, to experience the joy of God, we have to first experience something less than joyful. That is why the world is important. Without it, God would not be able to experience the joy of his/her nature. Therefore, through the world (Energy), God is known.

The Goddess said:

ⅽɜ 22 ɛɔ

O God of Gods, having a cup as an ornament and a trident as an emblem, devoid of direction, place, time and description.

ⅽɜ 23 ɛɔ

By what means can one acquire and be filled with that form of God? In what way is the Supreme Goddess, the entrance to God? O God, explain it to me in such a manner, that I may understand it fully.

The Goddess asks two more questions. *By what means can one acquire and be filled with that form of God?* In reply to this God gives 112 methods. The second question relates to how the Supreme Goddess is the entrance to God. The Goddess then wants the questions explained in a manner, so that she can understand it fully. Shiva does not answer the second question directly. But what an answer He gives! Instead of getting drawn into further philosophical discussions, He gives 112 methods to reach God. 112 techniques for uncovering the God within us. Words cannot explain Ultimate Reality, only experience can. Philosophical discussions can only take one thus far. To truly understand God, one has to reach God, become God. The experience is what is most important. It is only when we experience God that we fully understand Him.

When the Goddess asks God in Verse 23, to answer Her questions in a manner so that She can understand it fully, He does just that. But it is not the answer we expect. We would expect God to expand on the answers He has given in the previous verses. But God does not do that. Instead God shows us how to reach God, achieve liberation. Once we reach the state of God, then we will understand everything about God. It is not necessary to understand everything about God, before starting one's spiritual journey. It is important to start. Once we progress on the spiritual path, we will automatically understand and know more about God. Buddha gave a beautiful example to explain this. He said that if a man is shot by an arrow, the doctor will first try to save the man by pulling out the arrow, and then treat the wound. But if the man stops the doctor, and says, "Wait. I first want to know who shot the arrow, how the arrow was made, and what wood the arrow was made from" – then that man will die. Therefore, it is important to start one's spiritual quest, and not wait for all the answers before starting.

The way God answers the Goddess's questions (by giving techniques), underlines one of the major differences between religion and spiritualism. In religion, we are asked to accept other people's beliefs and experiences about God. In spiritualism, we are encouraged to have our own experiences of God. To enable us to do that, 112 different methods are given in this text.

God replies to the Goddess's questions by giving 112 meditation techniques. These techniques are for liberation. It is not necessary to understand every technique. It is necessary to understand and practice one technique. That one method will be sufficient for enlightenment. While reading these meditations, you will find a few that you are inclined towards.

You may experiment with these few, maybe practicing each for a week at a time. The one that takes you the deepest, or gives you the most peace or joy, is the technique for you. When you feel a sense of peace while practicing or even reading a meditation, you will know that that is the meditation for you.

CHAPTER 2

THE MEDITATIONS

O Arjuna, all human beings in every way,
pursue a path to Me.

—Bhagavad Gita (4:11)

Some of the meditations given in this text can be described as "sitting" meditations. In these particular meditations, one has to sit (usually with eyes closed) and practice a particular meditation technique. There are certain guidelines for practicing these techniques, which are given at the end of the book. These guidelines are common for all sitting meditations.

God said:

∞ 24 ∞

The Supreme Energy (breath) goes upwards with exhalation and downwards with inhalation. By concentrating on the two places of its origin, one acquires the state of fulfillment.

Many meditation techniques attempt to quieten the mind, by first focusing the mind on a single point. It is easier to still the mind, by first concentrating the mind on something, than by not concentrating on anything. The breath has been known to be one of the easiest ways to concentrate the mind. That is why the meditations involving breath have been given first.

This verse and the next three verses are asking us to concentrate on the gap between two breaths. There is a gap between our inbreath and our outbreath. There is another gap between our outbreath and our inbreath. We are to focus our attention on these two gaps. This is what is meant by *concentrating on the two places of its origin.* The breath originates from this pause.

Sit in a comfortable posture and close your eyes. Focus your attention on your breath. Then focus your attention on the gap between two breaths. Do not try and influence your breath in any way. Just observe it. You must try and maintain continuous awareness – of the breath and more particularly, the gap between two breaths. You should not make the mistake of only concentrating on the gaps between breaths, and letting the mind wander during the breath. If one does that, then one will also miss the gap between two breaths. Therefore concentrate on the full breathing cycle, with increased focus on the gap between the breaths.

As you do this practice, you may find the breath becoming more subtle and refined. The gap between two breaths may also increase. The breath may slow down. The entire breathing cycle may lengthen. When this happens, the mind may calm down. As you continue this practice, you will feel a sense of peace, then joy.

Why is the origin (the gap) of the breath so important? The breath is pure energy. She is the Supreme Goddess Herself. She originates from God and returns to God. By concentrating on Her origin, one is concentrating on God Himself.

25

Concentrate on the two places where the breath turns from inside to outside and also from outside to inside. O Goddess, in this way, through the Goddess, the essential form of God is realized.

This meditation is a slight variation of the previous one. Instead of focusing on the origin of the inbreath and the outbreath, focus on the turning of the breath. As you breathe in, the breath gradually dies out. Then there is a small gap or pause, and then you breathe out. Turning of the breath is the area where the inbreath is ending, there is a gap, and then the outbreath starts. The focus of attention in this verse is larger. It encompasses not just the gap between two breaths, but also a little on either side of it – where the inbreath is ending and the outbreath is beginning and also where the outbreath is ending and the inbreath is starting. In a complete breathing cycle, the breath turns twice. From inside to outside and again from outside to inside.

Like the previous verse, this technique should be practiced seated, with eyes closed.

People have wondered for centuries, what is it about the breath that makes it such a powerful meditation technique. When people fail to keep the mind quiet with other meditations, they usually succeed with one of the breath techniques. The mind is attracted to rhythms. It is easier to focus the mind on a rhythm. And the breath is the most natural rhythm found in life.

These meditations bring the mind to the present moment. The mind always takes us to the past or the future. In the present, the mind cannot exist. In the present, there is no need, no use of the mind. One is only aware. By focusing the mind long enough on the present, the mind automatically dissolves.

While practicing these meditations, thoughts may keep popping up. When a thought arises, we miss the turning of the breath. Do not get upset when this happens. Simply, bring the mind back to the practice. Do not dwell on the thoughts that have arisen, or get upset that these thoughts keep arising. Bring the mind back to the meditation. Gradually the thoughts will diminish, and one day will be eliminated altogether.

Through the Goddess, the essential form of God is realized. The Goddess is breath or Energy. Through Her, or through breath awareness we reach God.

26

At the Center where the breath does not enter or the breath does not go out, all thoughts disappear. The form of Energy becomes visible, and through her the form of God appears.

Verse 26 is not a separate meditation practice. It is the same meditation that has been given in Verse 24. It is repeated again for emphasis. This is because it is a very important practice. It is a simple and powerful technique for stilling the mind.

When we are still, silent, we reach God. At the center, at the gap between two breaths, we are completely still. We are not even breathing. By being aware of that middle state, that stillness, all thoughts disappear. Because our body is completely still at that time, our mind also becomes still. When our mind becomes still, the form of God appears. When we look at a calm, serene lake, our mind automatically becomes more peaceful. The serenity of the lake makes our mind more tranquil. This is why the center or gap between two breaths is so special. In that state, in that moment, our body is completely still. By focusing our mind on that stillness, our mind also becomes still.

Do not try and intentionally hold the breath. Allow the body to breathe normally. Focus your attention on the breath, and pay complete attention to the gap between two breaths. Try not to miss a single gap. As you do this practice, you will find yourself breathing more slowly, more softly, more gently. This happens automatically, without any effort. The length of your breath may increase. You may now be breathing fewer times per minute. As you become aware of the stillness, the gap between two breaths, the mind becomes more and more still. Fewer thoughts will arise, and you will start feeling more peaceful and joyful. That is what is meant when the verse says the *form of Energy becomes visible.* Finally, if the mind is stilled long enough, one reaches the state of enlightenment.

These techniques are simple to understand. Do not let the mind fool you into thinking that because they are simple, one will not achieve liberation through them. Truth is always simple; it is never complex. The meditations involving breath may be simple, but they are very, very powerful. That is why they are given first.

The Kashmir masters used to emphasize this meditation. The gap between breaths is special. It is a moment of complete stillness. And it is in stillness that we find God. It is in that gap, that stillness that we can more easily reach God.

☙ 27 ❧

When by itself the breath is retained after inhalation or exhalation – then in the end, through Energy known as peace, Peace is revealed.

The verse refers to a situation, where our breath automatically stops after inhalation or exhalation. For this to happen, we first have to practice a breathing meditation. It could be either of the three previous meditations, or it could be simple awareness of the breath.

Sit comfortably, close your eyes, and focus your awareness on your breath. Gradually your breath will slow down. You will be breathing in and out more gently and slowly. The cycle time of your breath will increase. It will take you longer to complete a full cycle of breath. We normally breathe in and out (one cycle), 15 times a minute. This will now slow down. As the span of your breath increases, you breathe fewer times per minute. With awareness of one's breath, this may happen automatically. Otherwise, one should try and breathe slowly and deeply.

When we start breathing more slowly, the mind calms down and we begin to feel more peaceful. When we breathe slowly, our breath becomes more subtle, more light. Immediately we feel more relaxed, more peaceful. Gradually, the span of each breath keeps increasing. It takes us longer to breathe in and longer to breathe out. The gap between breaths also keeps increasing. The breath becomes subtle and more subtle. Finally, a stage may come when the breath stops altogether. That is the stage this verse refers to. What happens next varies from person to person. Some may hear a sound, others may not. Eventually, Kundalini, the dormant energy lying near the base of the spine, rises upwards through the central channel of the spine. As she rises, one feels a deep sense of peace. When she reaches the top of the head, one becomes liberated.

The length of the breathing cycle has a direct effect on the life of a living being. Animals that breathe faster than humans (more breaths per minute) have a shorter life span. Those that breathe slower than humans live longer. For example, if you observe the breathing pattern of dogs, you will find that they breathe extremely rapidly. They also have much shorter life spans than humans. On the other hand, tortoises breathe very slowly, and live longer than human beings. When we breathe slowly and deeply, we immediately feel more relaxed and peaceful. This does not mean that we should practice deep breathing 24 hours a day. However, deep breathing can be very useful as a meditation practice, and is also strongly advised when one is feeling angry or tense. It immediately makes one more calm and tranquil.

ॐ 28 ॐ

Meditate on the energy in the form of a bright ray of light, rising from the root energy center, becoming subtler and subtler, until finally dissolving at the highest center. Then God appears.

The next two verses are about raising *Kundalini* – the energy that is lying dormant near the base of the spine. One could write books on Kundalini, chakras and the channels. However, what follows is a brief description of the terms, sufficient to enable one to understand the next two meditations.

Yoga and tantra maintain that we have a subtle body apart from our gross body. The subtle body cannot be seen by the naked eye. However, it is vitally important. Without it, the gross body would not exist. The subtle body comprises of chakras and channels. Chakra means wheel. A chakra is basically an energy center. There are seven important chakras. Their location in the body is given in the diagram. The mooladhara chakra is located near the base of the spine. In the male body, it is located near the perineum, between the penis and the anal passage. In the female body, it is located at the root of the uterus, in the cervix. Swadhisthana chakra is located at the base of the spinal column, at the level of the tailbone. Manipura chakra is located directly behind the navel, inside the spinal column. Anahata chakra is located directly behind the point just below where the rib cage meets, in the spinal column. Vishuddhi chakra is found in the spinal column, directly behind the throat pit. Ajna chakra is located at the top of the spine. It extends horizontally forward to a point between, and just above the eyebrows. Sahasrara chakra is located at the top of the head.

LOCATION OF CHAKRAS

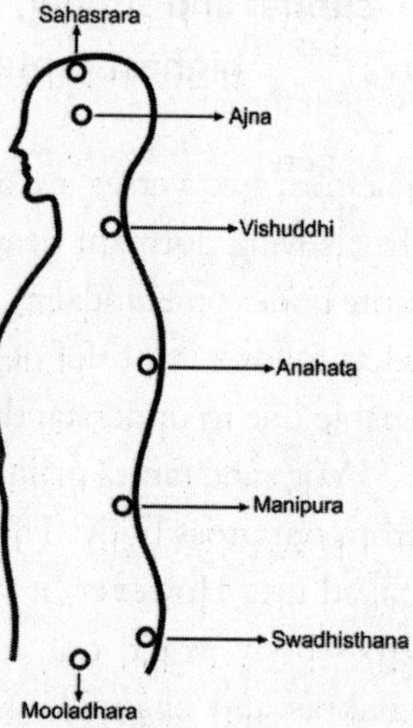

Our subtle body also has several *nadis* or channels. There are three that are important, and of these three, one is of primary importance. That one is *Sushumna Nadi* or the central channel. Sushumna starts from Mooladhara chakra, and extends upwards through the inner channel of the spine upto Ajna chakra. From there it extends upwards to Sahasrara chakra, and terminates there. With the exception of the last chakra (Sahasrara), all the other chakras are located inside this channel.

Kundalini is dormant energy that is lying at the Mooladhara chakra. It is sometimes symbolized as a serpent lying coiled three and a half times around a *Shiva lingam*. Many meditation practices attempt to free this dormant energy. When this energy is freed, it rises up the spine, through the central channel (Sushumna), piercing each energy center (chakra). When it finally reaches the crown chakra (Sahasrara), an individual is liberated. At this point, the energy is said to have reunited with God. It is called the union of the God and the Goddess, Shiva and Shakti. The union of Consciousness (God), and Energy (Goddess). The *Vigyan Bhairava* was originally part of a text called *Rudrayamala Tantra*. Rudrayamala means exactly this. The union of God and Goddess (Shiva and Shakti).

A more accurate way to describe this process would be to say that the energy and consciousness within us, has united with the energy and consciousness outside us. Individual Energy and Consciousness has reunited with Universal Energy and Consciousness. God within us has reunited with God outside. The great Indian saint Kabir, gave an example to explain this. He said that if you dip a pot into a body of water, the pot gets filled with water. Now, if the top of the pot is kept above the water level, the water inside becomes separate from the water outside. To get the water inside the pot to rejoin the water outside, break the pot. Then, there will be water everywhere. The ascent of Kundalini, the freeing of this energy is nothing but the individual energy and consciousness rejoining Supreme energy and consciousness. God within us reunites with God outside. Then there is only God everywhere. Just as in the example, when you break the pot, there is water everywhere, now there is God everywhere. That is why Self-Realized Masters see God everywhere and in everything. Their "pot", their ego or sense of separate identity, has been broken. Even if a person tries to harm a Saint, she only responds with love. This is discussed in greater detail, later in the book.

In Verse 28, we attempt to raise this energy (Kundalini), through a process of visualization. The central channel (Sushumna) should be visualized as a white or translucent tube. The chakras each have their colors and form. In some traditions, they are symbolized as different petalled lotuses, and in the Kashmir tradition, they are shown as wheels. For the purpose of the next two meditations, it is sufficient to visualize each chakra as a round ball of light.

Sit comfortably with your eyes closed, and focus your attention on the root chakra (Mooladhara), situated at the base of the central channel. Now, imagine a ray of light rising from this chakra, up the spine, through the central channel (Sushumna), piercing each energy center. As it pierces each energy center, it becomes subtler. Like this, the ray of light continues upwards, getting fainter and fainter, until finally dissolving at the crown chakra. Initially, while doing this practice, it is useful to mentally say the name of each center, as the light pierces it. Mooladhara, Swadhisthana, Manipura, etc.

You must be focused on this ray of light as it rises up the spine, piercing each center. After it rises and dissolves in the highest center, start again from the root center. Imagine another ray of light rising upwards, piercing each center successively. Continue this for upto 30 minutes.

Then God appears. God appears when the Kundalini energy finally rises through the central channel, to the top. This union is a feeling of complete bliss.

☙ 29 ❧

Meditate on the energy in the form of lightning, ascending from energy center to energy center till the highest center. In the end, experience Great Love rising.

The meditation given here is a variation of the previous one. Instead of imagining a ray of light continuously rising up your spine, see it rising in flashes, like lightening. It jumps from center to center successively upwards till Sahasrara, the highest center. Unlike the previous verse, this light does not get subtler and subtler as it rises. When the light reaches the highest center, start again from the root center. Your awareness must continuously follow this light.

In the end, experience Great Love rising. When Kundalini finally begins her ascent, there is a great feeling of love. As she rises, the feeling of love keeps increasing. When she reaches the top center, one is liberated. Then one experiences an ocean of love. One becomes love, one is love – pure, unconditional love.

Releasing energy from matter is always very powerful. This is basically the theory behind the atom bomb. Releasing energy from the human body liberates us. There are several meditations in yoga similar to the last two. Much of Kriya yoga is based on visualization of the chakras, and on moving one's awareness up and down the various channels in the body. However, these meditations that directly try to raise Kundalini are very powerful. Sometimes, they can even be dangerous. The guidance of a master is always advised. These last two meditations are relatively safer than some of the other similar meditations found in yoga. But if you ever feel any discomfort while practicing these last two meditations, then stop the practice immediately. Seek the help of a master, or instead practice any of the other 110 meditations given in this text.

☙ 30 ❧

Meditate successively on the twelve Sanskrit letters. First in a gross form. Then leaving that aside, in a subtle form. Then leaving that aside, in a supreme form. Finally leaving them aside, become Shiva.

The meditation given here is to help us go into the void – into silence. However, this is done in stages. Instead of directly diving into silence, we are lead there gently. This is to help us go deeper into silence.

The 12 Sanskrit letters referred to are the vowels – a ā, i, ī, u, ū, e, ai, o, au, am and ah. First, *look* at the vowel. That is what is meant by meditating on it in a gross form. Next, say the vowel out loud. That is meditation in a subtle form, through sound. After the sound ends, there will be a subtle vibration or *feeling* of the sound. Concentrate on that. This is meditation in a supreme form. Finally, there is silence. Meditate on that silence. After this go to the next vowel, and repeat this four-stage process – first look at it. Then, say it out loud. Then, observe the subtle vibrations or feeling as the sound ends. Finally, and most importantly, meditate on the silence after the vibration ends. Spend the maximum amount of time on this stage, concentrating on the silence. Maintain awareness throughout this process.

Finally leaving them aside, become Shiva. There is a dual meaning here. First we are to become silent (like Shiva), and meditate on the silence. This is the last stage of the meditation practice mentioned above. God is found in the silence. This is one of the important teachings of yoga. There are other techniques given in the text that lead us into silence. The second meaning of the line above is to become liberated. To become God, or to uncover our true nature.

ଓ 31 ୨

Concentrate without thoughts on a point between and just above the eyebrows. The Divine Energy breaks out and rises above to the crown of the head, immediately filling one completely with her ecstasy.

The point between and just above the eyebrows is a very significant point for meditation, in yoga. This point is called *Bhrumadya*. It is sometimes represented as the third eye. *Bhrumadya* is the front part of Ajna chakra, a very important energy center. It is said that when the third eye opens, we gain insight into the inner world. This is an ancient practice, and a very important one. It is the only meditation given by Lord Krishna in the Bhagavad Gita.

The movement of the eyes is connected to the thought process. When we think the eyes move, and when the eyes move, we think. One of the quickest, most direct ways to stop thoughts from arising, is to stop the eyes from moving, even from blinking. There are other meditations in this text that employ the same method – of focusing the eyes without movement, on a particular spot. Some of the meditations are with eyes open, while some are with eyes closed. In this verse, a very powerful spot has been chosen for focusing our sight – the front part of Ajna chakra.

The meditation is to be done seated with eyes closed. It is a mistake to believe that when the eyes are closed, they do not move. They in fact keep moving, as we think. When you are sitting comfortably with eyes closed, focus your gaze upwards, to a point between and just above the eyebrows. Because the eyes are closed, you will only see darkness. But, identify the point between your eyebrows, and maintain your awareness there. You will find this spot easy to identify. The third eye waits for our attention. Your eyes are naturally drawn to this place.

If you are successful in maintaining your gaze on that spot, you may see a blue or white light appearing there. The minute that happens, you will be filled with ecstasy. Do not wait for the light to appear, or be disappointed if it does not appear. Different people have different experiences during meditation. The important point is to focus on Ajna chakra *without* moving your eyes. You will go very deep in your meditation, and will have an experience unique to you.

The Divine Energy breaks out and rises above to the crown of the head, immediately filling one completely with her ecstasy. This is a reference to Kundalini, the dormant energy, rising up the spine to the top of the head. When this occurs, one is liberated.

☙ 32 ❧

Meditate on the five voids in the form of the five colored circles on a peacock's tail. When the circles dissolve, one will enter into the Supreme Void within.

The five voids is a reference to the five senses. The senses of touch, taste, sight, hearing and smell. One is to meditate on the five colored circles found on a peacock's tail. These circles represent the five senses.

Look at a picture of a peacock's tail. Now focus your awareness on the five circles on the peacock's tail. Keep looking at them without moving or blinking the eyes. If your eyes feel tired, or start watering, close your eyes. After a while, open your eyes, and continue with this practice. A time will come when the circles dissolve. The circles disappear because the mind has *disappeared.* Without the mind, it is not possible to see anything. The mind is like a data processor. It processes the input received by the eye into the final image that we see. Without the optical center in the brain, one would not be able to see anything. When the mind disappears, momentarily, the forms we are looking at disappear.

When the circles dissolve, one will enter into the Supreme Void within. When the circles dissolve, the mind disappears, and one is liberated. The Supreme Void is another name for God. God is found within. When the circles dissolve, the mind disappears, and our true nature unfolds. One enters God, or one becomes God.

In this meditation, one has to look at the circles on a peacock's tail. One has to look continuously till the circles disappear. At that point, one achieves enlightenment. Because the circles disappear, it does not mean that we become blind, or cannot see anything. It only signifies the point when the mind disappears. This text uses the terminology of the mind disappearing or dissolving, very often. This does not mean that the mind no longer exists. What it means is that the mind is now under our control. We can use it whenever we want to and not use it when we don't. In most people, the presence of the mind is felt continuously. One is always thinking, moving from thought to thought. This inner chatter never dies out. When the text says the mind disappears, it means that we have become internally silent. The mind's presence is no longer felt continuously. The inner chatter has finally ended. In the context of this meditation, the circles dissolve and the mind disappears. The circles then reappear, but now everything has changed. The mind is gone (or is under our control), and one is now free, liberated. It is like a person who always lived in a small village. He knows nothing of the outside world. He then gets a chance to travel and see the whole world. When he comes back to the village, he is a changed person. The village may be the same, but now he is different. He has grown. His experience has broadened his vision. Similarly, when the circles reappear, the outside world may be the same, but now you are different. You are now liberated.

☙ 33 ❧

Similarly, by gradually focusing one's attention on anything, whether on space, or a wall, or a great person, one is completely absorbed into the Supreme Reality.

The meditation of Verse 33 is similar to the previous one. It is based on the same principle, and is probably easier to practice. Instead of concentrating on the five circles on a peacock's tail, concentrate on anything. Concentrate on space, a wall, a picture of a great person, or on any other object.

To practice concentrating on space, one has to look at space in front of the eyes, without blinking the eyes. After a while if the eyes tire, close them for a short period. Then open the eyes and continue with the practice.

Similarly, one can practice on a wall. There are two ways of doing this. First, one can sit in front of a plain white wall, which has no marks on it. This is a very powerful practice. Because there are no other objects, the mind dissolves very fast. Our ego needs another object to survive. We get our separate sense of identity by looking at other objects, and seeing ourselves as different from them. But what if there are no other objects to look at? There is only a plain white wall. Then our sense of separateness, our ego, dissolves. We become one with the Whole. The second way to practice this is to look continuously at a dot on a wall. Keep looking at the dot or point without blinking. Gradually, the point starts fading. That is when the mind starts fading. When the point completely dissolves, the mind completely dissolves, and one is absorbed into the Supreme Reality.

This meditation can even be practiced on the picture of a great person. Use a picture of Krishna, or Christ, or Buddha, or some other great person you respect. Keep looking at the picture continuously without moving or blinking the eyes. One can use any object for practicing this meditation. Choose an object you are familiar with, something you enjoy looking at. It will be easier to maintain your concentration on such an object.

by gradually focusing one's attention on anything. When you stop the eyes from moving, even blinking, you stop the flow of thoughts. This is how all "looking" techniques work. When you initially practice this meditation, you may find it difficult to keep the eyes open for an extended period of time, without blinking. The eyes may tire very quickly, and you may have to close them. After practicing for a while, you will find that you can keep the eyes open for longer periods of time. The longer you keep the eyes open without blinking, the longer you remain without thoughts, and the closer you come to realizing your true nature.

∞ 34 ∞

Seated with eyes closed, fix one's attention inside the skull. From firmness in concentration, one will gradually perceive the Supreme Reality.

All meditation practices lead us to the unity in all life forms. Our sense organs do not give us the complete picture. They show us a world of diversity and movement, without showing the underlying unity or stillness behind the external world. When we open our eyes, we see different forms and objects, and the movement of certain objects. When we close our eyes and fix our attention inside the skull, we see only darkness. There are no forms or objects visible in the darkness. There is only darkness. Similarly, when we close our eyes, there is no movement whatsoever. There is only stillness.

This is a simple meditation practice that takes us to a place beyond our sense organs. A place of unity and stillness, and a place where we meet God. Sit comfortably and close your eyes. Focus your attention inside the skull, to the area behind the forehead. Concentrate on the darkness there. After a while, you may see some images. Observe them and let them pass. If thoughts arise, ignore them and continue with the practice.

From firmness in concentration, one will gradually perceive the Supreme Reality. As we continue with this practice, gradually our thoughts become less and less. Eventually, they are eliminated altogether. It is when our concentration becomes unwavering that we start perceiving God. We are able to focus on the area behind the forehead with fewer thoughts arising. That is when we gradually start perceiving God. When thoughts stop completely, then we reach God.

When you practice this meditation, you realize how wonderful it is to be in a state without thoughts. Initially, you may be in this state only for short periods of time. Just closing the eyes, focusing on the darkness behind the forehead, and being still, makes one feel at peace. When you close the senses and shut out the noises of the external world, you are quickly led to the peace within. More than external noise, it is the internal chatter of the mind that disturbs us. By focusing the mind on darkness and stillness, we make the mind still. As the mind becomes still, we first feel a deep sense of peace. This peace turns into an incredible feeling of joy. Even if this peace or joy is experienced for brief moments of time, it becomes an experience that one longs for. It is an experience that nothing in the outside world can match. We then come to realize something very important – the greatest joy we can experience, we experience within ourselves.

ଓ 35 ଠ

The central channel located in the middle of the spinal cord has the appearance of the lotus thread. Meditate on its inner space. The Goddess then reveals God.

The central channel is the Sushumna nadi described in Verse 28. It extends from Mooladhara chakra at the perineum, up the center of the spine, to the top of the head. It is as delicate as a lotus thread. Usually it is visualized as a thin, white or translucent tube. One has to meditate on its inner space. Start from the base and move slowly upwards. Take your awareness inside this channel, and move up this passageway. Notice the inside wall of this channel as you move upwards. When you reach the top, start again from the base and move upwards.

In this practice, it is not necessary to visualize any of the chakras or energy centers located in this channel. One only has to meditate on the inner space of this passageway. The central channel is very important in yoga. It is the basis of many meditation techniques. When Kundalini is freed, it rises to the top of the head through the central channel. When it reaches the top of the head, one achieves enlightenment. The central channel is therefore, literally the road to God. It is the path taken by Kundalini, the dormant energy. In this meditation, we are literally treading the path to God. We are moving our awareness up this path, up this channel. We are walking on the road to God. If you walk on the road to God, you reach God.

The Goddess then reveals God. The sentence refers to the ascent of Kundalini. By practicing this meditation, by moving our awareness up this channel, Kundalini breaks out from Mooladhara chakra, and rises up the central channel to the top of the head. When this occurs, the Divinity within us is revealed, and we reach our Highest State.

Most of the past few meditations direct our awareness within. That is because God is found within. The external world is temporary. It does not bring us eternal happiness. When we base our happiness on something external, we experience disappointment. That is because all things in the external world are temporary. They all suffer change and pass away. Money, success, sex, or holidays will not bring us lasting happiness. When we go on vacation, we come back relaxed and peaceful. But we do not remain peaceful for the rest of our lives. Something similar also happens when we buy something, such as an expensive car, or a new house. The happiness we experience from the new purchase is temporary. It soon fades away. The Katha Upanishad states this beautifully, when it advises us not to seek the eternal in things that pass away. On the other hand, the joy we find within is permanent. It is always there. It needs nothing external to exist. When we discover this joy, we find an eternal source of joy. External events no longer trouble us. That is why masters are always calm, even in the face of a calamity. They know that a crisis will also pass. But the joy within will remain with them forever.

☙ 36 ❧

By concentrating on a point between the eyebrows, a light will be seen. Then, with the fingers of the hand, close the seven openings of the senses in the head. The light will gradually dissolve, and one will then permanently reside in their highest state.

The meditation of Verse 36 is initially very similar to the meditation of Verse 31. One has to sit with eyes closed and concentrate on a point between and just above the eyebrows. It is important to avoid moving the eyes. One has to focus completely on the point between and just above the eyebrows. After some time, one may see a light there. Then to hasten the process of enlightenment, one performs *Shanmukhi Mudra.*

Shanmukhi Mudra

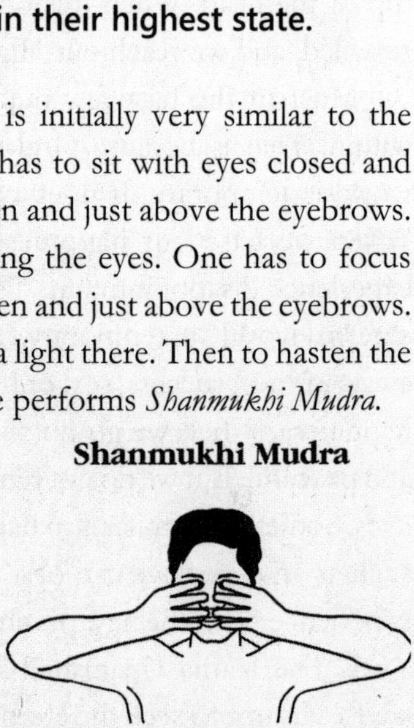

In Shanmukhi Mudra, we close the seven openings of the head with the ten fingers of the hand. The arms may be kept parallel to the ground. The forefingers close the eyes, the thumbs close the ears (by pressing the ear flap against the ear opening), the middle fingers close the nostrils (by pressing the outer part of the nose against the inner), and the ring finger and little finger close the lips, by resting above and below the lips respectively. Although the eyes were closed, we still put the forefingers at the base of the eyelids.

The openings of the head are to be closed in this way, only after a light is seen between the eyebrows. When we close the openings of the head, we direct our awareness with greater force within, to the light between the eyebrows. The external environment is now completely cut off. This makes the light dissolve faster. When the light dissolves, we permanently reside in our highest state.

Closing the nostrils, we are not able to breathe. Ordinarily we would start suffocating. However, after the light appears, the breath is already suspended. The nostrils and the other sense organs can then safely be closed.

37

Press the eyes gently. A subtle light resembling a dot will appear at the top of the head, or in the heart. Absorb oneself there. From this meditation, one is absorbed into the Highest Reality.

Sit comfortably, and close the eyes. Now, press the eyes gently. A subtle light like a dot will appear in either of two places inside the body – either at the top of the head, or in the region of the heart. Concentrate deeply on this light. Become one with this light. Gradually all thoughts will disappear. Then, one will be absorbed into God.

A flame of light or a dot of light is used frequently in yoga for meditation. It is a very powerful method for focusing the mind. The mind is easily attracted to light. It is possible to concentrate for long periods on light. There is a yogic practice called *Trataka*, where one has to look at the flame of a candle without blinking. In this verse, one looks at an internal source of light. The dot of light appears either at the top of the head or in the heart. This happens because when we press the eyes, the optic nerve gets stimulated. A spark of light then appears. Because it appears inside the body, it is surrounded by darkness. There is just a dot of light, and darkness all around it. It then becomes easier to concentrate on it. When you focus the mind completely on this light, the mind becomes silent. After that, one reaches God.

38

Bathe deeply in the continuous sound of a river flowing, or by closing the ears, hear the unstruck sound of God. One will then realize God.

The sound of a river flowing is a natural sound. It is also a continuous sound. In this practice, one has to immerse oneself completely in this sound. All other sounds are to be blocked out. It is best to practice this meditation with eyes closed. One has to sit near a river and close one's eyes. Because the sound of a stream flowing is natural, it is soothing. It is unlike some of the sounds we hear in a city, that are disturbing. As the sound is soothing and continuous, it makes the mind more tranquil. It is easy to absorb one's mind there. Become immersed completely in this sound. Become totally absorbed in this sound. Then the mind will become more calm and peaceful. All thoughts will end and one will realize God.

or by closing the ears, hear the unstruck sound of God. Normally a sound is made by striking two objects together. An unstruck sound is one that occurs spontaneously. It is not caused by one object striking another. An example of an unstruck sound is the sound of one's breath. This sound is a natural sound that continues throughout one's life. The practice of listening to one's breath is an extremely important one, and is given at the end of this text. There are certain cosmic sounds that the ancient yogis heard while they were deep in meditation. These cosmic sounds are also unstruck sounds. Some of these cosmic sounds are given below.

The greatest unstruck sound of God is the sound of silence. It is often said that God is found in silence. By focusing the mind on silence, the mind becomes *silent.* By focusing the mind on stillness, the mind becomes *still.* In this practice, we close the ears to block out all external noise, and concentrate on the silence within. By being aware of the silence, the mind automatically becomes silent.

When we are in a noisy environment, where car horns are blowing, or people are shouting, the mind becomes disturbed. We become tense, or easily agitated. On the other hand, when we are in a serene, peaceful environment, the mind becomes peaceful. If you are looking at the sea, or some beautiful mountains, the mind automatically relaxes. That is why people love looking at the sea. A calm, peaceful sea immediately relaxes a person. The mind slows down. Fewer thoughts arise. That is what this meditation does. By being aware of the silence, the mind becomes more peaceful, and it becomes more silent.

When we close the ears and concentrate on the silence, we sometimes hear certain cosmic sounds. These cosmic sounds are also unstruck sounds. If you hear any such sound, focus on it. Once it goes away, concentrate again on the silence. Yoga says, there are ten internal sounds one may hear. The sounds indicate that one is progressing towards God. However, it is not necessary to hear these sounds in order to realize God. Being aware of the silence is sufficient. The ten sounds are:

a) Sound of a bee humming.
b) The sound of the word "Chini".
c) The sound of bells ringing.
d) The sound of a conch shell.
e) The sound of a vina or stringed instrument.
f) The sound of cymbals.
g) The sound of a flute.
h) The sound of a drum echoing.
i) The sound of two drums.
j) Finally, the sound of thunder.

☙ 39 ❧

O Goddess, chant AUM, etc., slowly. Concentrate on the void at the end of the protracted sound. Then with the supreme energy of the void, one goes to the Void.

The *Maitri Upanishad* teaches us that God can be meditated on in two ways – through sound and through silence. From sound, we go to silence. The sound of God is AUM. The silence after AUM is joy. It is the joy of God. The meditation given in this verse is almost exactly what is taught in the Maitri Upanishad.

Sound and silence are two sides of the same coin. Sound is the opposite of silence. Because it is the opposite of silence, it is used as a springboard to go deeper into silence. For example, there are two ways of relaxing our body. First, we could straightaway try and relax our body. Make every part of our body, every muscle limp and relaxed. Second, we could initially tense our body. Tighten every muscle of our body to the best of our ability, without excessive straining, and then suddenly relax and let go. In the second instance, our body would relax automatically. Maybe even relax more than the first method. This is the basic principle followed in this and the next two verses – through sound go deeper into silence. In the silence, we will meet God. This verse is doubly powerful. Not only does it use sound to go into silence, but the sound it uses, AUM, is by itself sufficient to take us to God. Therefore, the meditation works in two ways – the sound takes us to God, and the silence also takes us to God.

O Goddess, chant AUM, etc., slowly. This meditation is to be done seated with eyes closed. *Etc.*, refers to two other sacred sounds of God – Hum and Hrim. One has to slowly chant either of the three sacred sounds of God, Aum, Hum or Hrim. There are only three sounds we can make without moving the tongue. When the mouth is open, we make the sound aaaaa. When the mouth is partially closed, we make the sound uuuuu. When the mouth is fully closed we make the sound mmmmm. Therefore, AUM is the only sound we can make without moving the tongue. Chant AUM by opening the mouth and making the sound aaaaa. As we close the mouth, the aaa sound will become uuu and when the mouth is fully closed, the sound will become mmm.

Concentrate on the void at the end of the protracted sound. Concentrate on the void or silence at the end of the sound. The meditation must be done in a quiet place, where there is no distraction due to external noises. Otherwise, one will not be able to concentrate on the silence. After a while, repeat this process. Chant AUM slowly, and then concentrate on the silence after the end of the sound. A point may come when one is completely absorbed in the silence. At this stage, there is no need to chant AUM again. Maintain your awareness of the silence.

Then with the supreme energy of the void, one goes to the Void. By concentrating on the void, the silence, one will start feeling very peaceful, and at times, very joyful. A time will come when one is transported to another level. One feels a deep sense of peace and bliss. At that time, one goes to the Void – one goes to God.

☙ 40 ❧

Concentrate on the void at the beginning or end of the sound of any letter. Then by the power of that void, one will become the Void.

Paramahansa Yogananda was a Self Realized Yoga Master of India, who lived in the latter part of the 19th century, and the first half of the 20th century. He was responsible for spreading the practice of yoga in America, particularly a variety called Kriya Yoga. Yogananda emphasized the importance of silence. He used to teach that silence was the altar of God, and that conversation with God requires silence. Being aware of silence is a very important way of stilling the mind.

The meditation given in this verse is a variation of the previous one. Instead of using the sound AUM, any sound can be used. Choose a sound that you love. That will help you in your meditation. Now chant this sound. Concentrate on the void, the silence before the sound begins or after the sound ends. Continue with this practice. You will find yourself going deeper and deeper into silence. As you do so, you will become more and more peaceful.

by the power of that void, one will become the Void. The void, the silence, will make the mind silent. Ultimately, the mind will become completely silent. All thoughts will stop. At that stage, one will become the Void, one will become God.

Most of the sitting meditations make one very peaceful. Whether it is the breath meditations, or the meditations using sound and silence, or any other meditation. The peace one feels needs to be experienced. It is not something that can be easily described or experienced in the outside world. Once a person has experienced it, she longs for a repeat of the same experience. A person starts looking forward to practicing her meditation. It also changes the person completely. You remain calm and peaceful for the rest of the day. External events do not trouble you anymore. Simple things start bringing you joy – going for a walk in the park, or spending time with your family. You no longer find it necessary to keep switching on the computer or looking at the mobile phone. You are happy even spending time with yourself, alone. You are peaceful. And you are happy being alone, being peaceful.

41

Listen with undivided attention, towards the end of prolonged sounds of stringed and other musical instruments. By staying with the gradual diminishment of the sound, one will obtain the form of the Supreme Space.

The sound of stringed and other musical instruments are beautiful. They attract our attention easily. This allows us to concentrate on these sounds continuously. They also have another advantage – they gradually diminish. Usually, even after the sound ends, the echo or vibration continues in our mind for some time. As a sound becomes more and more subtle, our awareness becomes greater and greater in order to hear the subtle sound. After the sound ends, our awareness increases further, in order to catch the subtle vibrations that continue. Finally, the vibrations end in the void, the silence. By this time, our awareness has increased greatly.

This practice should be done with eyes closed. Choose an instrument that you enjoy listening to. Listen to the sound of somebody else playing your favorite instrument. If that is not possible, play the stringed instrument yourself. Play it a few times and then put it down. Listen to the sound of the instrument gradually diminish. When the sound ends, listen carefully to the subtle vibrations that continue.

One can also do a variation of this practice. Once the sound and the vibration ends, there is only silence. Continue to be aware of the silence. By listening to the gradual diminishment of the sound, one's awareness increases greatly. This increased awareness is carried over into increased awareness of the silence. One is now more aware of the silence then one would have been if one had straightaway meditated on the silence.

One will obtain the form of the Supreme Space. Supreme Space is God. One will obtain the form of God.

42

Chant AUM audibly. Gradually the sound diminishes. By concentrating on the point where the sound ends into the void, one becomes Shiva.

The meditation given in this verse focuses on increasing degrees of subtlety. In that sense, it is similar to the meditation of the previous verse. The sound AUM should be chanted audibly and slowly. The sound gradually diminishes. It should be chanted so that the M component in AUM continues for some time – mmmmm. After the sound ends the vibration continues for some time. Finally, the vibration ends in silence. Focus on the point where the vibration of the sound ends in silence - the junction point between sound and silence. It is a subtle point, and needs increased awareness to notice it. Once you are aware of this point, your awareness increases greatly.

Because one is chanting the sound, it is easier to maintain awareness. If one was listening to someone else chanting, the mind could start wandering, and awareness would be lost. As one is saying the sound themselves, the mind becomes more attentive.

Continue with this meditation by repeating this process – chant AUM audibly, and slowly end the sound. Focus on the point where the sound vibrations end in silence. The mind will become still, and one will become Shiva.

43

With mind free of thoughts, concentrate on one's body. Imagine space simultaneously pervading in all directions. One will then become all pervasive.

The *Ashtavakra Gita* is one of the most beautiful and enlightening spiritual texts in the world. Its importance has not yet been fully appreciated. There was an incident in Ashtavakra's life when he was only 12 years old that is very significant. It helps explain the next six verses.

Ashtavakra was born deformed. Some scholars say he was deformed in eight places. His father was a renowned scholar. He was an upper caste brahmin, well versed in the Vedas, and other religious texts. King Janak had organized a debate in his court. He offered fabulous prizes to the winner. Scholars were invited from all over the kingdom. The debate was on truth, and other religious topics. Ashtavakra's father defeated several scholars. However, in the final round, he started losing to another scholar. Someone rushed to Ashtavakra and informed him that his father was losing the debate. Ashtavakra immediately went to King Janak's court.

When Ashtavakra entered the court, the scholars saw him and started laughing. They saw the eight deformities in his body and how ridiculous he looked when he moved, and they could not stop laughing. Amazingly, Ashtavakra started laughing too. King Janak then asked Ashtavakra, "I can see why the scholars are laughing, but I cannot understand why you are laughing." Ashtavakra replied, "I came here to see a conference of scholars, but instead I see a group of *Chamars* (cobblers), debating truth." The court was stunned into silence. Here was a 12 year old boy, calling these upper caste brahmins and scholars, a group of low caste cobblers. Janak asked Ashtavakra to explain himself. Ashtavakra replied, "These people only see skin. They judge me by my body. They do not look within. It is difficult to find someone more pure and truthful than me. But these people do not see that. They see the body and not the soul. That is why they are only shoemakers. They work with leather and skin. If a pot is broken, is the air inside the pot also broken? My body is deformed, but I am not. Look within me, you will find someone pure and truthful."

King Janak was extremely impressed by this reply. He said nothing at that moment, but sought out Ashtavakra the next day. On meeting Ashtavakra, he immediately asked him three questions – "How does one attain wisdom, detachment and liberation?" Ashtavakra's reply is the *Ashtavakra Gita*.

It is impossible to say how much of what reportedly happened in King Janak's court is true. But it does convey a very important message – we are not our body. This is a message the Ashtavakra Gita makes repeatedly. In fact, in the very first page (Verse 4), the Ashtavakra Gita makes a remarkable statement. It says that if we can detach ourselves from our body, and rest in our own awareness, we will be free this moment. *This moment.* Very few texts make this statement. But first, one has to detach oneself from the body. Believe that one is not the body, but awareness. If you can do this now, you will be free this very moment. If you cannot, the next six verses show you how to detach yourself from your body.

With mind free of thoughts, concentrate on one's body. Imagine space simultaneously pervading in all directions. Sit in a comfortable posture, and close your eyes. Focus your awareness on your body. Imagine there is no body – only space, pervading in all directions. Practice this for upto 30 minutes, or for as long as you are comfortable.

One will then become all pervasive. Our true nature is to be unlimited, free, and all pervasive. The body is what binds us. When we believe we are not the body, then we become liberated – we become all pervasive.

44

Meditate simultaneously, on the above as void and the base as void. The Energy that is independent of the body will make one devoid of thoughts.

Identification with our body is the problem. This identification causes us misery. When we are no longer identified with the body, we become blissful. We become a witness. You are simply aware of what your body is saying or doing. You are also aware of how others are responding to what your body is saying or doing. Because you are no longer identified with the body, you are no longer affected by what happens to the body. If people are rude to you or strike you, it does not upset you. You are not affected negatively by any of the adverse events that occur in your life. You reach this stage in your evolution, when your level of awareness increases. You become aware, and suddenly you become aware that you are aware. By being aware, you discover your soul – the witness in you. You start identifying more with this witness, and less with your body. As this happens, you become peaceful, and the external world starts losing its hold on you.

Ramana Maharshi was a fully enlightened saint, who lived in South India. He became well known during the first half of the 20th century. He eventually died of cancer. The doctors who diagnosed him as suffering from cancer were amazed at his condition. He should have been feeling a lot of pain, but he felt none. He had an abundance of joy and love flowing from him. Being enlightened, he no longer identified with his body. The pain of the body was no longer his pain. He remained joyful through every moment of the day. What was happening to his body, no longer affected him.

The next few verses are all trying to break our identification with the body. The body is there, it exists. But we are not our bodies. We are awareness. We are the witness, who observe all the events of our life.

Meditate simultaneously, on the above as void and the base as void. The above refers to the part of the body that is above the shoulders. That is from the neck upwards. The base refers to the lower part of the body, from the waist down. This meditation differs from the previous one, in that we are to simultaneously concentrate not on the whole body, but on two parts of it. Now, we are to imagine these two parts of the body to be void, empty or nonexistent. The meditation should be practiced seated with eyes closed. Focus your attention simultaneously on the two parts of the body – from the neck upwards, and from the waist downwards. Imagine that these two parts of your body do not exist. There is only space or emptiness there.

The Energy that is independent of the body will make one devoid of thoughts. Energy is in the body. It is because of this energy that the body exists. However, this energy is independent of the body. It is the energy of God, and does not require the body to exist. Through this practice, we raise Kundalini, our dormant energy. Then our awareness grows, and all thoughts stop.

☙ 45 ❧

Meditate firmly and simultaneously on the above as void, the base as void and the heart as void. Then, by being free of thoughts, will arise the state that is permanently free of thoughts.

The meditation given in this verse is a slight variation of the previous one. In the previous meditation, one had to consider the top of the body and the lower part of the body as void. In this practice, the area of the heart has also been added. Therefore, one has to simultaneously consider the top of the body, the base of the body and the area of the heart to be void, empty.

Sit comfortably and close your eyes. Focus simultaneously on the three areas of your body – from the neck upwards, from the waist downwards, and the region of the heart. Consider these three areas to be empty, non-existent. Continuously believe these three areas do not exist. Instead, there is emptiness there. Once you are completely absorbed in this meditation, you will be free of thoughts. When your body and mind is empty or void, then who is there that can think? Once you are without thoughts for a period of time, you become permanently free of thoughts.

Several meditation practices bring one's attention to the present. In the present, the mind stops thinking. There is only awareness. Gradually, the number of thoughts start decreasing. The gap between thoughts starts increasing. A time will come when thoughts stop altogether.

When you believe you are not the body, then who are you? You are awareness, consciousness, the witness or the observer, who observes what the body is doing or thinking. These practices detach us from the body. They lead us directly into awareness. When we realize we are not the body but consciousness, we become aware.

Our ego is our sense of separate identity. It is our identification with name and form rather than with universal consciousness. These verses are trying to change this. Instead of identifying with name and form, we are to identify with consciousness. We still carry on activities in this world through our body but no longer claim ownership for it. Our sense of doership disappears as our ego disappears. A master may still achieve great things in this world, but he does nothing. All things merely happen in his presence.

Tantra says that we all seek pleasures, and try to avoid pain, and that is why we suffer. That is also why we are obsessed with money and success. We believe that with money we can increase our pleasures and lessen our pain. However, pain is unavoidable. Pain and pleasure come together. You cannot have one without the other. Even a rich and successful person will have problems.

Tantra says the way to avoid suffering is not to avoid pain, (which is impossible) but to break the identification with the body. One has to give up the "I am the body" idea, and instead identify with the witness within them. When you are able to do this, no external event, no matter how terrible, will be able to affect you. Whatever is happening, is happening to your body and not to the real you. The real you, the observer, remains unaffected by all external events. Once you are able to do this, you will find great peace. Something similar happens when we watch a movie. Sometimes, when we watch a movie, we become completely engrossed in it, and react emotionally to what we see on the screen. Then, suddenly we become aware of ourselves watching the movie, and our whole attitude changes. We relax and enjoy the movie, without being affected by it. It is the same with life. Once we become aware of our Self, we watch the passing scenes of life, without being affected by them.

Not being attached to the body is a great freedom. It frees one from the tensions and stresses of life. One is not bothered by what one has achieved or not achieved. Whether one has succeeded or failed. The achievements of the body are no longer of primary importance. As a witness, as consciousness, one observes the ups and downs of life with an equanimity that was not present earlier.

46

Free of thoughts, consider for a short while, any part of one's body as only void. One becomes permanently free of thoughts. Then, one's own form attains the splendor of the state that is free of thoughts.

In this practice, one is to consider any part of the body as void. Choose a part of the body that you find easy to meditate on. It could be the nose, a finger, the chest, or any other part of the body. Then sit comfortably, close your eyes and consider that part of the body to be void.

The body is a unit. All parts are interconnected. If a particular part has a certain property, then the entire body has that property too. If a particular part of the body is void, then the entire body is void. Some people may find it difficult to meditate on the entire body as void. They may find it easier to concentrate on a small part of the body. In either case, the effect is the same. If a part of the body is void, then the entire body is void.

Free of thoughts. This is an important point. While practicing any sitting meditation, one has to focus on the practice. If one is thinking, then one is not meditating; one is only thinking. While meditating, thoughts may arise. Sometimes one is lost in a train of thoughts. When this happens, a person should not get frustrated of upset. Instead, bring your awareness back to the practice. The moment you realize you are thinking, stop the thoughts and focus again on the practice.

The last few verses have been described as sitting meditations. They do not necessarily have to be practiced that way. Some of them can be practiced throughout the day. British spiritual master Douglas Harding had a mystical experience in the Himalayas, several years ago. He suddenly felt he had no head. Only two eyes peering into the universe. His mind had stopped working, and he felt a sense of unity with everything. Time no longer existed, and there was only the present moment. He described his experiences in a book called, *On Having No Head: Zen and the Rediscovery of the Obvious.* It was an experience he tried to instill in his students. You can try this yourself now. Imagine you have no head. Someone or something has cut it off. What would you be then? There would be no thoughts, as there would be no mind. You would simply be aware, living in the present, from moment to moment.

You experience this feeling of headlessness, when your awareness grows. Suddenly, you stop identifying with your body. You feel that your head and your body is nothing; it is empty, void. Instead, you feel this infinite expanse of space, and that you are one with this space. You feel one with all of life, and your sense of self literally, grows to infinity.

Then, one's own form attains the splendor of the state that is free of thoughts. When a person becomes enlightened, they emanate a sense of peace and joy to all those who come into contact with them. People who met Mahatma Gandhi or Mother Teresa always remarked how they felt a feeling of love and compassion flowing from these great saints. Being in their presence was enough to feel the love they always gave. People visit places where the great masters lived. Jerusalem where Christ preached, Dwarka where Krishna lived, and Bodh Gaya where Buddha attained enlightenment. The vibrations of these Masters are still felt there centuries after they've passed away. There is a sense of peace that still prevails in these places.

47

O Deer eyed one, consider all the constituents of one's body to be pervaded by empty space. Then, one will permanently become settled in that conception.

Our thoughts create our reality. What we are today is the result of our past thoughts. What we will be tomorrow, will be the result of our present thoughts. This is an important truth that is emphasized in the *Upanishads,* the *Ashtavakra Gita,* and the Buddhist *Dhammapada.* Some of the techniques in this text use the mind to change our thoughts and beliefs. The new thought or new belief helps us to revert to our true nature. The new belief is actually a very important spiritual truth. When practiced continuously, the new belief removes the layers of conditioning, and uncovers our True Self. These new beliefs actually go against what we are seeing. Yet they describe Reality the way it actually is. A motto used by most people is – seeing is believing. Spiritualism reverses this motto. Our seeing is the result of our believing, or rather a result of our beliefs. Yoga teaches that to see True Reality, change your beliefs. Once you change your beliefs, you see the truth.

For centuries, people thought the world was flat. Sailors were scared to sail too far, because they might fall off "the edge." When our knowledge increased, we realized what we were seeing was not true. The earth was actually round. Spiritualism is like that. When our awareness increases, we literally see more. When our beliefs change, we see more. We now see the truth. Verses 43 to 48 are subtly trying to change our beliefs. Our belief that we are our body. This belief is being changed to two other beliefs: we are awareness, and we are all pervasive, like space. We are not limited to a particular place. There are some beautiful verses later in the text that introduce us to new beliefs. New beliefs that if practiced, open the door to Eternity. This verse can also be practiced as a sitting meditation. Close your eyes and imagine all the internal elements of one's body to be filled with empty space. Whether it is the heart, liver, brain, muscles, tissue, or any other organ; consider all these to be pervaded by empty space. Inside a heart there is only space, inside muscle there is only space, inside the brain only space, and so on.

Then, one will permanently become settled in that conception. Then we permanently become like space. We become all pervasive. In other words, we become God.

48

Consider the skin to be the wall of an empty body with nothing inside. By meditating like this, one reaches a place beyond meditation.

Consider the body to be an empty shell, which has nothing inside. The skin is just an outer covering like a wall. Only air inside and air outside. Only God inside, and God outside. Then, one no longer identifies with the skin, with the body. One identifies with awareness, or the God inside. The Ashtavakra Gita says, because we think we are the body, we are bound. Once we believe we are awareness, we become free. When we believe that the body is nothing, it is empty, then we no longer believe we are the body. That is what this meditation is doing. If we consider the body to be empty, we realize that the body is insubstantial. Then we no longer believe we are the body. We are something more substantial, something more permanent. This verse is also suggesting a subtle truth. Our body really is nothing. It is insubstantial.

When our attachment to our body goes, our ego dissolves, and we become free. It is our identification with our body that makes us feel that we are separate from God. Because we see ourselves as separate, we are bound. When we no longer think of ourselves as our body, we no longer consider ourselves to be separate. We become free. It is like the example of air inside a pot and air outside a pot. When the pot breaks, the air becomes one. Similarly, when our identification with the body breaks, we are no longer separate from God. We become one with God.

By meditating like this, one reaches a place beyond meditation. Meditation is a means to an end. It is a means to liberation. It is not an end in itself. Once a person is liberated, they no longer need to practice meditation. By meditating like this, one is liberated. Then meditation is no longer required. One has reached a place beyond meditation.

☙ 49 ❧

When the senses are absorbed in the inner space of the heart, one should concentrate with undivided attention on the center of the two bowls of the lotus, located there. Then O Beloved, one obtains the Supreme Fortune.

This is a practice for finding God within, in one's own heart. Close your eyes and sit comfortably. Now focus your attention inside the body, in the region of the heart.

When the senses are absorbed in the inner space of the heart. When your concentration is so firm, that you are no longer distracted by the senses. You hear no external sound or disturbance. You are completely and fully absorbed in the inner space of the heart. Then, at that point, you will see two lotus flowers inside your heart. A lotus flower is shaped like a bowl. You will see two lotuses on top of each other, one facing up and one facing down. Then, move your awareness inside these two bowls or lotuses. Maintain your concentration continuously in the space inside these two lotuses. Then, suddenly you will find the consciousness of God rising in a flash. After that, you will be in a state of bliss. That is what the verse means, when it says, one obtains the Supreme Fortune.

God is love. The heart is considered to be the center of love in the human body. That is why this meditation uses the inner space of the heart to concentrate on. That is where we find love, and that is where we find God.

☙ 50 ❧

Absorb the mind completely at the end of twelve, within one's own body. When steadiness of intellect is firmly established, one's true nature is perceived.

There is a word used here, dvādaśānte, that needs to be expained. Dvādaśānte is made of up two words, dvādaśa and ante. Dvādaśa means twelve or twelfth and ante means, at the end of. The literal meaning of dvādaśānte is "at the end of twelve". Twelve refers to the width of twelve fingers. There are three places in the body known as dvādaśānte: the heart, the pit of the throat and the point between the eyebrows. As verse 55 makes clear, dvādaśānte refers to the heart. The heart is twelve finger widths from the base of the nose. The meditation practice is to absorb the mind completely at the heart. It is a variation of the previous meditation.

When steadiness of intellect is firmly established, one's true nature is perceived. This is true for all sitting meditations. Sometimes when we start a meditation practice, our mind keeps wandering. The benefits of the meditation practice are less in this case. Gradually, our concentration improves. We are able to maintain awareness for longer periods of time. Our mind becomes calm, and fewer thoughts arise. Our awareness keeps increasing. The mind becomes more and more steady (fewer thoughts), until finally all thoughts stop. Then, our true nature is perceived.

☙ 51 ❧

During every moment, in whatever way, in whatever place, one should fix one's attention at the end of twelve. The mind will be deprived of support and within a few days, one will be extrordinary.

This is similar to the previous meditation, except that it needs to be practiced throughout the day. It is usually not sufficient only to practice a sitting meditation for reaching God. Progress will be slow. While practicing a sitting meditation, one is trying to maintain awareness of the present moment. It is important to maintain this awareness, this meditative attitude *throughout the day*. Practicing a sitting meditation for half an hour a day, and then letting the mind wander freely for the rest of the day will not be effective. When we practice a sitting meditation, the mind is stilled to an extent. If we then let the mind wander freely for the rest of the day, most of the benefit of the sitting meditation will be lost. The next day when we practice a sitting meditation, we will be starting almost from zero. That is why it is important not only to practice a sitting meditation, but also to try and remain aware throughout the day. To try and keep the mind quiet for the rest of the day. Progress will then be very rapid.

in whatever way. Do whatever it takes for you to be aware of the heart. Be determined. Don't give up. The more firm you are in your intent, the more determined you are, the easier it will be for you to maintain awareness.

in whatever place. Wherever you are, whether you are having a bath, eating dinner, or talking to someone, remain aware of the heart. This is what meditation is really about. To be in a meditative state means to be aware. And one should be aware throughout the day. You will find it easier to be aware (of the heart, or anything else), when you are alone. Even if you are walking or driving a car. It becomes tougher to remain aware when you are talking to someone else. It becomes tougher still when you are watching a movie. In whatever situation you find yourself in during the day, you must try and remain aware of the heart. That is what this verse is teaching us.

The mind will be deprived of support. When something is not used, it becomes weaker. This is easily noticed in the case of the muscles of our body. If we fracture our left arm, the arm will have to be in a plaster for a few weeks. We will not be able to use the arm during this time. When the plaster is finally removed, one will notice that the left arm is a little thinner than the right arm. Since the muscles of the left arm were not used for a few weeks, they will be weaker than the muscles of the right arm. The mind works in a similar way. In order for the mind to exist the way it currently does, it has to continuously move from thought to thought. When the mind is not used, when the flow of thoughts is stopped, the mind becomes quiet on its own. By focusing the mind on the heart, we stop the mind from thinking. The mind needs thoughts to survive. When we stop the flow of thoughts, the support for the mind is gone. Then the mind on its own becomes quiet.

and within a few days, one will be extraordinary. Practices like this one, where we try and maintain awareness throughout the day, take us very rapidly to God. Sometimes even days are not required. In a few hours, or even minutes, one is free.

☙ 52 ❧

Imagine one's own body being burnt by a destructive fire, rising from the right foot, to the top. Then one will attain a calm splendor.

Verse 52 is another meditation which tries to break our identification with our body. It is meant to teach us a very important truth – we are not our body. This practice can be done seated or lying down, with eyes closed. Imagine a destructive fire rising upwards from your right foot, burning your entire body. When this fire reaches the top, your entire body is destroyed, but *not you.* You are still there even though the body is gone. You are now awareness or consciousness, something that can exist even without a body. There are two very important spiritual truths being taught here. Even when our body is destroyed, we survive. And our true nature is consciousness. Consciousness cannot be destroyed. Its survival is guaranteed. The entire practice can be repeated a few times.

Then one will attain a calm splendor. This practice detaches us from our body. When we realize we are not our body, our ego dissolves, our separate identity disappears. Then, we become free.

To live without fear is a great blessing. All sorrow comes from fear. Fear is usually the fear of loss of some kind. Loss of wealth, loss of life, loss of one's family, loss of job, loss of face, and so on. Fear of death is a major fear for most people. You have fear when you think your existence is in danger. When you realize you are not the body, you realize that you cannot be destroyed. Even when your physical body is destroyed, you will still survive. Death is something that happens to your body and not to you. When you know you cannot be destroyed, all fears melt away. That is when you truly love. Even when someone attacks you, you have no fear. Even when someone is about to kill you, you have no fear. For you know you cannot be destroyed. When there is no fear, there is only love, unconditional love. You love friends and enemies alike, for you know nothing of any value can be destroyed.

Mahatma Gandhi was one such man who lived life fearlessly. He was one of the first to protest against the apartheid regime of South Africa. He is better known for having won India its independence from the British Empire. The amazing thing about him was that all his methods of protest were *non-violent.* His revolution was based on non-violence. He did not hate his colonial masters or wish them any harm, no matter how repugnant their behavior became. He had an unconditional love and respect for all of human life. Once when he was threatened with violence, he said, "You can beat me, you can torture me, you can even kill me. Then, all you will have is my dead body. Not my obedience."

53

Similarly, meditate with undivided attention, that the entire world is burnt by fire. That person then attains the highest state.

Verse 53 is a variation of the previous verse. It is a sitting meditation to be practiced with eyes closed. Instead of imagining one's own body being burnt by fire, imagine the entire world being burnt by fire. You can start with one particular area, country, or continent. Now visualize that area being burnt, along with every form on it. Visualize this fire spreading everywhere, burning everything existing on this planet. Every form, inanimate or living, burning. Finally, visualize your own body and the place you reside on fire.

Even though the entire world and your body is destroyed, you still survive. Your survival is guaranteed. It does not depend on this world or on your body. You are part of God, and you can never die. This is a practice that helps us detach from our body and this world. It helps us realize our true nature – consciousness. We are the witness that watches the world or our body being destroyed. It is this state of awareness, of being a witness that we must carry forward from this meditation, to our everyday lives. Be an observer, a witness of all the events that unfold in your life, knowing that even the worst possible outcome – the destruction of the entire world (and your body), has no material effect on your existence. When you realize this, your mind becomes calm and you rest in awareness. That is why masters are calm even in the face of a calamity. They know that the entire world may pass away, but they will not.

This verse has a great deal of practical wisdom that can be put to use in our everyday lives. Everyone faces problems in their lives. Most people do not enjoy dealing with them. Some get tense and upset in the face of a mounting problem. Now, if you came to understand that your survival is guaranteed, you would see your life in an entirely different light. Even if this world is destroyed, with everything on it, you will still survive. With this long term perspective, you will face problems with a different attitude. You will remain calm and peaceful in the face of any disturbance in your life.

More importantly, one should be aware during all the events of one's life. That is what this meditation is really teaching us. We are not the body or the "doer". The body does things. The real "I" is not the body. The real "I" is the observer, the witness, who is aware of what the body is doing or not doing. By continuously being aware, we reach our highest state. We reach full awareness.

☙ 54 ❧

Meditate that the constitutive elements of one's own body, or the world are becoming subtle and more subtle, until they finally disappear. In the end, the Supreme Goddess is revealed.

In the previous two verses, one had to concentrate on either the body or the world being destroyed by fire. In this meditation, one has to imagine that the body or the world slowly disappears. The end result in these three verses is the same. The body or the world no longer exists. The process given in this verse is different. It is slower and more subtle.

Sit comfortably and close your eyes. Concentrate on either the body or the world. Now imagine it slowly dissolving. For example, if you visualize the world, imagine its constitutive elements slowly fading. You may start by visualizing a particular town or countryside. Now imagine all the people and the houses in that place slowly fading. They start becoming less firm, less solid, less real. This process continues until everything finally disappears.

When everything has disappeared, you are still there. That is what is important. You are the witnessing consciousness that survives the dissolution of the world.

In the end, the Supreme Goddess is revealed. The Supreme Goddess is no different from God. In the end, our highest state is reached. We become one with the Goddess or God.

☙ 55 ❧

Having entered the heart and meditated upon the energy that is gross and subtle, abiding in the twelfth, the meditator obtains freedom and liberation.

This is similar to the meditation given in verse 50 and 51. One has to focus one's attention on dvādaśānte, on the heart. The energy referred to here is the breath. The breath may be gross or subtle. It may make a sound or if we are breathing slowly and deeply, the breath will be subtle. The mediation practice is to focus on our breath at the heart.

Most people falsely believe that unless their lives are free of problems, they cannot be happy. That in fact is the problem. Our happiness or joy, does not depend on anything external. People also believe that if they had more money, they would be happy. With money they could solve or eliminate most of their problems, or fulfill their desires, and then they would be happy. Actually, problems continue even when one has money. They do not go away even for rich people. Yoga teaches that happiness does not depend on money or a problem free life. One can be happy or unhappy with money, and one can be happy or unhappy without money. Similarly, one can be happy or unhappy with or without problems. Our happiness depends on the mind. With the mind, one can never be fully joyful. Without the mind, one can only be joyful; one can never be unhappy. The lesser the activity of the mind, the more aware and joyful one becomes. When the mind has completely disappeared, one becomes fully aware and totally joyful.

◆ 56 ◆

Consider the form of the entire universe being dissolved successively from the gross state to the subtle, and from the subtle state to the supreme, until finally one's mind is dissolved.

The world is part of God. It flows out from God. Now, one has to imagine this process being reversed. Just as a wave subsides back into water, a pot dissolves into clay, or a bracelet dissolves into metal, meditate that the entire world dissolves into God.

Practice this meditation sitting comfortably, and with eyes closed. Imagine the entire world or the universe slowly dissolving. First see it as a solid object. Then imagine it becoming liquid. After this, as gas or vapor. Finally, there is only space. When there is nothing left, only space, there will be awareness. Everything has dissolved into consciousness. You will be aware of this empty space, and aware of *yourself* being aware. At this stage, there is only one Observer, and that Observer is God. Nothing else exists. This meditation shows us Ultimate Reality the way it actually is. There is only God, and God is aware, and aware of Himself or Herself being aware. In the final stages of this meditation, you are just like that. There is nothing else. The universe has dissolved. There is only you being aware. And you are aware that you are aware.

until finally one's mind is dissolved. This meditation helps us identify with consciousness. We have two selves within us. There is our mind that keeps on thinking. This is our ego-self. Our ego is not real. It is something insubstantial, like a shadow. Then there is awareness – the witness within us, who observes all the events of our life. This is our Real Self. This verse helps us identify with the witness in us, not with our mind or ego. As we start identifying more with consciousness, our mind starts dissolving. Eventually, our mind disappears altogether.

In this practice, the world and everything in it is being dissolved. Your body, your separate identity is also dissolving into One. When your separate identity dissolves, your mind also dissolves. In the end, when everything is gone, there is still consciousness. Everything has dissolved into consciousness. Consciousness is the Supreme State. God is Consciousness. Consciousness or awareness is the True Reality underlying the entire universe.

☙ 57 ❧

Meditate that this entire universe all round upto its end limits, is part of Shiva. By meditating in this manner – the Great Awakening.

Buddha used to say that a vehicle is body and wheels arranged in a particular way. A fist is fingers and hand arranged in a particular way. In the truest sense, a vehicle or a fist is not a separate entity. It is a temporary arrangement of certain parts. In the same way, the universe is not a separate entity in the absolute sense. *It is an arrangement of God in a particular way.* That is what this verse is saying to us here. Just as a fist is not a separate entity, but a temporary arrangement of fingers and hand – in the same way the universe and everything in it, is part of God. It is God arranged in a particular way.

In the previous verse, one had to imagine the universe slowly dissolving into its pure state – into God. Using the fist example, that would be similar to watching the fist slowly opening. In the end, the fist is gone, and there is only fingers and hand in its original state. In this verse, one does not have to see the universe dissolving. One has to meditate on the universe as it currently is – as a part of God. God shaped or formed in a particular way. It is like seeing a fist for what it truly is – nothing but a particular arrangement of fingers and hand. Therefore, the universe does not exist as a separate entity. It is part of God. It is full of God. It is only God shaped in a particular way.

So, sit and meditate on the universe. Visualize it not as a separate entity, but as a part of God, as a form of God. See it as being filled with God. See every part of the universe being filled with God. Just as air fills a pot and flows around it, imagine God filling the universe completely and flowing around it.

58

O Great Goddess, one should consider this entire universe to be a void. Then the mind will dissolve and one will be absorbed into the Void.

This is the first technique regarding void or emptiness. There are a few others, later in the text. This is a concept also found in Buddhism.

What does *shunya*, emptiness or void really mean? When the verse says one should consider the universe to be empty; empty of what, one could ask. Empty of a separate self, empty of a separate existence, that is what emptiness or void means. Emptiness is also applied to human beings and to all objects found in the universe. Everything is empty of a separate self, but full of God. That is the meaning of emptiness in this tradition. Because nothing has a separate existence, but is only full of God, everything is interconnected. Everything is One, everything is God. This is one of the foundations of the non-dualistic tradition of yoga and tantra. The universe and everything in it does not exist as separate entities. They exist only as a form of God.

This particular verse can be practiced as a sitting meditation, or as a thought or belief one holds throughout the day. The meditation given in this verse, is a variation of the previous one. In the previous verse, one had to meditate that the universe was empty of a separate existence, and part of God. In this verse, one has to meditate that the universe is just empty. It does not exist as an entity. It is nothing. When this meditation is practiced as a belief, something one genuinely starts believing in, then it can be very powerful. This verse is stating a truth about the universe. It is not real, it is an illusion. It has no separate existence. When you start believing this, you change dramatically. When you know that what you are seeing is nothing, how can you prefer one thing to another? Nothing matters. You stop worrying about problems. You are no longer attached to results. Your desires are no longer addictive – that you must have something, or you must achieve something. You may still have goals and try and reach them, but you no longer mind if you don't achieve them. The stress and tension in life disappears.

Verse 58 is not just changing our belief about the world, it is changing our perception of the world. It is changing the way we perceive or look at the world. There are other meditations in the text that also change our perception. Sometimes when you change your perception or the way you look at something, your understanding grows. For example, if you perceive the world by standing in it, you will think the world is flat. Now if you were able to go into outer space and look at the world from there, you will realize the world is round. By changing the angle or the way we look at something, we are able to understand more.

Changing our perception is a very powerful way of stilling the mind. If it works for you, it can produce results very quickly. Sometimes, within a few minutes, the mind is stilled.

When you perceive or know the world is nothing, then what is there to think about? It is all nothing. All our thoughts are about this world, or the events taking place in it, particularly in our lives. When you know that the entire world and everything happening in it is nothing, that none of it matters, then why would you think? You would not. Then your mind dissolves and you start living in the present.

one will be absorbed into the Void. Void here means God. One will be absorbed into God.

☙ 59 ❧

Look at a bowl or any other vessel, without seeing its partitions. From the moment one is absorbed into space, one will be full of space.

Look at the space inside a bowl. Try and see only the space and not the bowl. The side and the base are the partitions of the bowl. One has to concentrate on the space inside the bowl, without seeing the base or the side of the bowl. Initially, one may see space and the bowl. Gradually the bowl may become fainter and fainter. There comes a moment when the bowl disappears, and one only sees space. That is the moment the mind disappears, and one is liberated.

From the moment one is absorbed into space, one will be full of space. This is the moment one only sees space. Absorbed into space means, only space is seen. The bowl has disappeared. *one will be full of space.* One becomes all pervasive. When a person is liberated, they are no longer limited to the body. They become all pervasive like space. Just as space exists everywhere, they too exist everywhere. A liberated person no longer feels separate. They feel one with all of creation. They realize the truth of their nature – that they are One with everything. That is why they are all pervasive. They now exist everywhere.

In Reality, there is only One. There is no division. Through the senses, we see division. The moment we are liberated, we see the unity in all things. We don't see any division. The mind is our main data processor. The mind processes the data received by the eye, and then we see objects. The moment the mind disappears, the object we are looking at disappears. That is why the bowl disappears, and we see only space. After a few moments, the bowl again reappears, but by then one is liberated.

All "looking" techniques such as these, should be done after removing spectacles or contact lenses. They should also be done without blinking the eyes. If the eyes feel tired, close them for a brief period. Then reopen the eyes and continue the practice.

☙ 60 ❧

Cast one's sight on a vast open place, with no trees, mountains, walls, etc. When one's mind has completely dissolved, one is born anew.

Our true nature is infinite. It is our mind and ego that limits us. In this meditation, one attempts to break the limitations imposed by the mind, by looking at an infinitely large area. The mind cannot exist with the infinite. Its very nature is to create limits, boundaries, definitions. In this practice, one is looking at a vast area, with no boundaries, trees, mountains or limitations of any kind. There is nothing to define it by. There is nothing for the mind to process. The mind also needs an object to think about. Thoughts cannot arise without an object. The mind cannot think of nothing. Then, it will not be thinking, it will be silent. In this meditation, there is no object in this place to look at. Nothing by which one can define this place – there are no mountains, rivers, villages, walls, etc. There is nothing. Without the support of a concrete object, the mind dissolves.

Two factors are used in this meditation to dissolve the mind. First, the place is vast, almost infinite. The mind needs something finite, or limited to survive. Second, there is no object to look at. The mind needs an object to think, it needs an object for support. By focusing on the infinite, one becomes infinite. Limitations imposed by the mind are broken. One grows beyond the ego or limited self. Because there is no object in this place, the mind stops thinking. Once it stops thinking continuously for a short period of time, it stops thinking altogether. Then the mind comes under one's control. There are no further uncontrolled streams of thoughts flowing through the mind.

Not having an object to look at is important for another reason. When there is no object to look at, there is also no subject. Our ego needs an object by which to define itself by. When there is an object that is different from us, or separate from us, we can define ourselves in relation to that. For example, when we see another person, animal, or inanimate object, we define ourselves as different from that. However, when we look at a place that has no object, there is nothing else to compare oneself with. There is nothing separate from us, because there is nothing else. *When there is nothing else separate from us, then we no longer remain separate.* Our ego dissolves, and we become one with the Whole. We become one with God.

When one's mind has completely dissolved, one is born anew. When one's mind has gone, one is a completely different person. It is like being born again. You lose your old habits, you old beliefs, your old identity. You have now become a new person. You are peaceful and joyful, irrespective of your external circumstances. You may face the same problems as you did earlier. But now your reaction to them is completely different. You remain peaceful even in circumstances that others would describe as unfortunate. People will notice this change in you. And some of them will certainly ask you about it.

ଓ 61 ଃ

When one has knowledge or perception of any two thoughts, one should simultaneously leave both aside, and reside in the center between the two. In the center, one's true nature shines forth.

When two thoughts arise together, one has to leave them both aside, and reside in the center between the two. What is in the center between two thoughts? Awareness is in the center. Between two thoughts, one is in a state of awareness. When one is thinking one cannot be aware, as one is lost in the chain of thoughts.

reside in the center. Reside in awareness. Remain in a state of awareness throughout the day. The *Vigyan Bhairava* is sometimes called a text on centering. Centering means to reside in the center, to live in awareness. Usually our attention is directed outwards to the world around us. When some of our attention is also directed back towards us, then we are in a state of awareness. We are aware of the self. The amount of attention that is directed to our self varies. Sometimes, the majority of our attention is inward and less outward, and at other times, the reverse is true. At least some attention should be directed to our self, even 1%. If no attention is directed inward, then a person is not in a state of awareness. They are lost in the external world. This frequently happens when we engage in a conversation with someone. We lose awareness of our self.

The Real Center is within us. It is within us that we find God, it is within us that we experience God. The senses and everything the senses perceive are at the periphery. In a state of awareness, we are aware of our self, which means we are aware of our Center. Awareness is our true nature. It is through awareness that we reach higher and higher states of awareness. When we are fully aware, we become God – *In the center, one's true nature shines forth.*

This verse asks us to leave aside two thoughts, when both these thoughts arise together. This happens rarely. We do not normally have two thoughts arising simultaneously. Usually it is a chain of thoughts. One thought follows another. From a practical point of view, the next verse is more relevant.

62

When the mind has left a thought, and is restrained from moving towards another thought, it comes to rest in the middle. Then, through that middle state of being, one's true nature blossoms brilliantly.

We normally think of time as consisting of past, present and future. In yoga, the present is not considered to be part of time. The present moment is the gateway to the eternal. The past and the future are part of time. And they are considered to be illusions. The past and the future do not exist. Only the present moment exists. Whatever event ever took place, only took place in the present, never in the past or the future.

When we think, the mind always takes us away from the present into the past or the future. It leads us into the illusion. When we are not thinking, then we are in a state of awareness.

We are living in the present. That is what awareness means – to live in the present, to be aware of the present moment. That is all the verse is teaching us. Stop thinking. Stop going into the past or the future. Remain aware, and live in the present moment. This is one of the central teachings of yoga. To live in awareness, to maintain a state of awareness throughout the day. When one practices a sitting meditation, one is attentive, one is in the present by following a meditation technique. Yet it is important to remain aware throughout the day, and not just for 30 minutes a day, while practicing a sitting meditation. This verse asks us to remain aware throughout the day. If a thought arises, leave it. Come back to the present.

Then, through that middle state of being, one's true nature blossoms brilliantly. The middle state of being is awareness. By being aware, by living in the present, one is liberated. It is one of the ironies of life that we find God in the present, in the Now. Usually we always look to the future for our salvation. This is true even of our everyday life. We believe we will only be happy in the future, after some event has occurred. After we have made some money, or after our children are settled, or after we go on holiday, or after we buy that house, and so on. The future is an illusion. It is a trap. There is no salvation there. Even after we make enough money, or buy that house, our lives do not change substantially. New problems arise, new challenges present themselves. It is only in the present that we find an abundance of joy. Buddha used to emphasize living in the Now, being attentive to the Here and Now. It was one of his central teachings. In fact, whichever path you choose, awareness in one form or another will always be required to reach God.

To practice this meditation, move deeply into the present. Turn everything you are doing into a meditation. Meditation simply means to be aware. If you are walking, be aware that you are walking. If you are having a bath, feel the water flowing into your body. If you are talking, observe yourself talking. Be fully attentive of the present moment, and watch everything it brings you. When you do this, you will immediately feel peaceful. *Immediately.* All tensions, all worries instantly leave you. You have no thought of tomorrow, what might happen or might not happen. When you live in the present, you are relaxed. You are not endlessly planning your day, thinking of the chores you have to complete, and how once you complete them, you can put your feet up and relax. Instead, you feel relaxed just by living in the present moment. By not worrying about the future, but simply enjoying fully the present moment, you feel a big burden has been lifted. A huge sense of relief is felt. All you have to do is just live in the present, from moment to moment.

A wonderful sense of peace and bliss is felt by living in the present. The mind is no longer active. You will then realize that the true cause of your suffering is the uncontrolled mind. Just by stopping the mind for a brief period, one feels so peaceful. If you find thoughts arising again, leave them and come back to the present. Living in the present is a wonderful experience. Once you practice this, you will never want to give it up. You will automatically find yourself living more and more in the present moment.

The question now arises, what should one do when one is facing problems. By living in the present, are we not avoiding the problems we are facing in our lives? Should we also not plan for the problems we might face in the future? The mind is a tool. It is meant to help us navigate the ups and downs of life. Should we not use the mind to solve our problems? Yes, the mind is a tool and can be used to solve problems. However, yoga teaches that a better way to solve problems is to go within. If you had a choice between the mind solving a problem, and God solving a problem, which would you choose? The mind is like a light bulb. It can shed some light on your problems. God is like the sun, giving infinitely more light than a light bulb. When you ask God for an answer, you get a perfect solution to your problems. So ask God for an answer, and then go within. You will be blessed with insight you never knew you had. You will receive the answer in a flash, in an instant. Sometimes you may receive the answer from external sources. In the next newspaper article you read, the next television program you watch, or the next conversation you have. All great discoveries have come through insight, in a flash. Even Einstein's Theory of Relativity. They do not come through lengthy reasoning of the mind.

It is also not necessary to think of problems that *might* arise in the future. The future is best left to itself. Sometimes when we face a problem, we dwell on future problems that may arise. For example, if a person loses their job, they may start thinking that they will go bankrupt, lose their house, or even face starvation. Usually various mental images occur along with these thoughts. These negative thoughts should be stopped immediately. There is no point thinking about a problem that has not yet occurred. When a problem arises, it should be dealt with at that time. Our thoughts create our future reality. By dwelling on negative thoughts, one only increases the likelihood of a negative outcome.

Even if one is facing an immediate problem, one should live in the present. See what you can do *now* to solve the problem. Instead of thinking of other problems that may arise, see what can be done now to find a solution to your existing problem. Worrying is a useless mental activity, that solves nothing and finds no solutions. It only damages your health. When you live in the present, you still the mind. It is only when the mind is quiet that you can find solutions to your problems. It is only when the mind is still, that we receive insight. Insight into our problems, insight that solves our problems. Therefore, in the face of any calamity, live in the present.

Problems are always a blessing in disguise. *Always.* A blessing that may not be appreciated till even years later. Problems are like a guide. They help us evolve and reach God. Buddha used to liken sorrow to a flash of insight. When there is a flash of lightening, we can suddenly see objects that were hidden in the dark. In the same way, sorrow is like a flash of insight into higher reality. It shows us the way home. Therefore, accept and trust whatever shows up in your life, knowing that each circumstance is perfect for you, and leads you to God.

When we live in awareness, we know intuitively that God will take care of us. That it is not necessary to worry and endlessly plan for the future. That whatever we need will be provided. In fact, this text and many others state that the higher one's level of awareness, the faster one desires are materialized. When we understand this, we immediately stop thinking so much about our lives. We are able to relax and live in the present moment. Therefore, trust God, have faith in God knowing that God always provides us with all that we need. This wisdom is found in other religions too. There is a beautiful passage in the Bible (St. Matthew 6:25-34), that explains this:

"Therefore I bid you put away anxious thoughts about food and drink to keep you alive, and clothes to cover your body. Surely life is more than food, the body more than clothes. Look at the birds of the air; they do not sow and reap and store in barns, yet your heavenly father feeds them. You are worth more than the birds! Which one of you, by being anxious, can add one thing to your life? And why be anxious about clothes? Consider how the lilies grow in the fields; they do not toil nor do they spin. Yet, I tell you, even Solomon in all his splendor was not attired like one of these. But if that is how God clothes the grass in the fields, which is there today, and tomorrow is thrown on the stove, will he not all the more clothe you? How little faith you have! No, do not ask anxiously, 'What are we to eat? What are we to drink? What shall we wear?' Therefore, seek ye first the kingdom of heaven, and all else will be added unto you. So do not be anxious about tomorrow; tomorrow will look after itself."

ଓ 63 ଓ

With mind free of thoughts, consider firmly one's entire body or the entire universe, to be consciousness. Then – the Supreme Awakening.

Our true nature is consciousness and joy. Yoga holds that all matter is nothing but energy. If you look deeper, you will find that behind energy, there is consciousness. This is a practice that can be done as a sitting meditation, or as a thought or belief one holds throughout the day.

As a sitting meditation it should be done with eyes closed. Focus your attention on the body or the universe. Imagine that the body or the universe in its present form does not exist. There is only consciousness or awareness.

With mind free of thoughts, consider firmly. Continuously believe that there is no body, only consciousness. That is the meaning of firmly in this verse. One has to believe continuously and one pointedly. There should be no wavering of the mind. This meditation leads us to an important truth – we are not our body, we are consciousness. The body is an important part of our ego. It gives us our sense of separate identity. When we disconnect from our body, our ego dissolves, and we become free.

This is also a meditation that can be practiced throughout the day. We are required to change our beliefs. Most spiritual texts teach that our thoughts create our reality. What we think, we become. This is mentioned in the Upanishads, the Ashtavakra Gita and the Buddhist Dhammapada. This also explains why Buddha used to teach that a wrongly directed mind would do us more harm than our worst enemy. Similarly, a well directed mind would do us more good than what our parents or our closest friends can. Therefore, it is more important to control our mind and change our beliefs, than to worry about our enemy or our best friend. Yet this is something very few people do. Most people would chase after some people, falsely believing that the key to their happiness lies in these other people, and what they can give them. People also worry about the harm their enemies can inflict on them. But the greatest harm inflicted on people is by themselves, not by others. This is done by their own minds and their self-limiting beliefs and thoughts. Similarly, the greatest happiness a person can receive depends on them, not on others. It lies in controlling the mind and in correcting self-limiting beliefs.

If you examine your own beliefs, you will find that they create your reality. If you believe people are basically dishonest or sinful, you will find dishonest and sinful people repeatedly coming into your life. To change one's life and to improve it, it is important to change one's beliefs. One has to reject negative thinking, and replace it with positive beliefs. For example, sometimes people worry about the lack of money in their lives. To improve their financial situation, one should first realize that God is within us. Therefore, the Source of all abundance is within us. How does one use this Source to create wealth in our external life? This is done by setting the mind aside. The mind creates limits. It tells us that we cannot make money because we are too old, or we do not have enough contacts, or we do not work hard enough, or there just isn't enough money out there for everyone. We have to reject and set aside these self-limiting beliefs created by the mind, and instead believe that anything is possible. One has to also stop thinking, and return to awareness. When we are aware and the mind is under control, all negative and self-limiting beliefs automatically disappear. One then creates results very fast. The greater one's awareness, the faster one produces results. When we are fully aware, we create results instantaneously.

Verse 63 gives us a belief that literally opens the door to eternity. We are given a thought about True Reality. The body and the universe are nothing but consciousness. When we start believing that we are not the body but consciousness, we become a witness. We become detached from what the body is doing or what is happening in our lives. We simply become an observer of all the events unfolding before us. We are no longer the body, we are awareness. Then the mind becomes still and we are liberated.

When one lives in awareness, one becomes joyful. Awareness is like a light in a dark room. The light shows objects that were previously hidden in the dark. In the same way, awareness brings out the joy that has always been present in us.

64

Concentrate on either of the two meeting points of one's breath – internal or external. The yogi will experience the birth of perfect understanding.

Being aware of the breath is a very direct way to still the mind. That is why there are so many breath techniques. Most of them are subtle variations of each other, to suit people of different temperaments. In this practice, focus on the breath, and then either of the meeting points of the two breaths. The inbreath with the outbreath or the outbreath with the inbreath. Instead of a gap between two breaths, some people may prefer to think of it as a junction or meeting point between two breaths. The junction between two breaths is a very subtle point. It requires increased awareness. This increased awareness of the breath and the junction point, stills the mind. Then, one is liberated.

ଓଃ 65 ୡ

One should consider one's entire body or the entire universe to be full of one's own bliss. Then, through one's own nectar of bliss, one will be full of the Supreme Bliss.

Joy and consciousness are our true nature. This verse is similar to Verse 63. In Verse 63, one had to believe that one's body, or the universe was consciousness. Here, one has to believe that one's body or the universe is full of joy; one's own joy, inherent in oneself. Like Verse 63, this can be practiced as a sitting meditation or as a belief held throughout the day.

Focus on the body or on the entire universe. Imagine either of them to be nothing but joy. Completely full of joy. This practice makes one feel joyful immediately. If you are concentrating on the body, instead of the body you feel there is only joy. If you are concentrating on the entire universe, the feeling is just the same. Your body is a part of the universe. In either case, you experience joy. Remain aware of this joy.

Maintain awareness on this joy. Ultimately, a time will come when one will permanently reside in joy.

When this meditation is practiced as a belief held throughout the day, spiritual progress will be very rapid. If you imagine your body to be full of joy, you will continue to remain joyful. Normally we are what we are because we are always responding to our external environment. Happy, sad, depressed, angry, joyful, etc. In this practice, one becomes *unconditionally* joyful. Joyful irrespective of one's external environment. The body is nothing but joy. Joy in every circumstance and every situation. When this meditation is practiced, extraordinary changes will occur in your life. You will discover people changing towards you, responding more positively towards you. You will find the more joy or love you give out, the more you will receive.

It is important to become established in one's own joy. Then one can be joyful unconditionally. That is what this verse is trying to do. It asks you to consider your own body or the entire universe to be *full of one's own bliss.* Joy or bliss is inherent in oneself. It is our true nature. It needs nothing external to survive. It is not dependent on external circumstances. Therefore, one can be joyful irrespective of our external situation. When we remain joyful, the mind becomes still. Instead of looking for joy or happiness outside, we have found it within. The mind stops thinking of the external environment. It falls silent. Then, one becomes totally blissful.

☙ 66 ❧

O Deer Eyed One, great joy arises instantly, while being caressed. Through that joy, one's true nature is manifested.

Sometimes, through our external environment, we experience joy. That joy is only a fraction of the joy of our Real Self. Nevertheless, that joy can lead us to the bliss of our true nature. In order for this to happen, we have to remain aware of the joy we are experiencing. Then, suddenly we will experience an explosion of joy, and our true nature will be revealed. This verse and Verses 68-74 are based on the same principle.

The sense of touch is different from our other sense organs. While being gently touched, one immediately feels pleasure. In this practice one has to be gently caressed, either by someone else or by oneself, on any part of the body. One instantly feels joy. Then one should be aware of this joy. One should remain aware of this joy. Joy is our basic nature. Whenever we experience joy, we come close to our real nature. That is why it is so important to remain aware of it. It leads us home to our Real Self. *Through that joy, one's true nature is manifested.*

The longer one remains joyful, the greater the chances of becoming liberated. It is not necessary to have an external stimulation for joy. As the previous verse suggested, one can just *be* joyful. But focus your awareness on the joy. If the mind is distracted by thoughts, then a person will not experience joy. She will be completely lost in thoughts.

☙ 67 ❧

By closing all the senses, the Energy of Life rises up gradually through the center of the spine, and one feels a tingling sensation like that of an ant moving on one. Utmost joy then spreads all over.

There are two interpretations of this verse. First, one can practice this as a sitting meditation. With the fingers of the hand, close the openings of the senses in the face. The thumbs should close the ears, the forefingers the eyes, the middle fingers the nose, and the ring fingers and the little fingers close the lips, by being placed above and below it respectively. From time to time, the middle fingers will need to be relaxed, so that the nostrils are opened and one can breathe.

By shutting the sense organs, consciousness cannot flow out. It is redirected to the center within. This causes Kundalini, the basic energy of life, to rise up through the center of the spine to the top of the head. When this energy reaches the top of the head, one is liberated. When Kundalini starts its ascent up the spine, a person feels a tingling sensation like that of an ant moving on one's body. Then, one feels the bliss of liberation.

This verse should be interpreted in a more general sense. *By closing all the senses,* means that one should not be affected by all the various inputs received from the sense organs. One should not be disturbed by what one sees, hears, smells, touches, etc. The great sage Patanjali in his *Yoga Sutras* described this stage as Pratyahara. It is a stage when the external world no longer affects you. It is a stage that every aspirant has to cross, in order to realize her true nature. Today, we would simply call it emotional control. In order to become one with God, we have to have control over our emotions. We have to attain detachment from the external world. It is a state of true freedom. The external world no longer controls us. We now control the external world. Normally we react to our external environment. If there are certain events taking place in our life that we like, we are happy. If there are events that we dislike, then we are unhappy. When people have control over their emotions, they are happy irrespective of their external circumstances. They are no longer reactive. They are now constant in their response to their external situation.

Emotional sensitivity is one of the main causes of suffering. The more sensitive we are to the external world, the more we suffer. This is applicable to everyone, irrespective of their social status or position in society. For example, film stars and sports athletes are amongst the most successful and famous people in the world. They have everything most people could ask for – fame and fortune. Yet, some of their personal lives are in shambles. This is because they are deeply attached to the senses, and the pleasures obtained through them. Then, one can react strongly to the external environment, specially when things are not happening as per one's expectations. When we have control over our emotions, we have control over our senses. That is when we have closed the doors of the senses, as the verse suggests. And that is when we realize our true nature.

How does one control one's emotions or detach oneself from the external world? There are many methods suggested in the text. One possible way is to understand that the greatest possible joy one experiences, one experiences within. This was mentioned earlier in Verse 15. The joy we find outside is nothing compared to the joy we find inside. Our joy or happiness is not dependent on external circumstances. Even if our external situation changes, we will always find a constant and abundant source of joy within. When we deeply understand this truth, we let go of our attachment to the outside world. We are able to live freely, knowing that whatever we need to be happy, we have within ourselves.

Detachment from the external world is important to achieve. If we are overly concerned with the external world, we will not be able to still the mind. It becomes difficult to detach from external events when we face a crisis. When we lose a job, or face a financial crisis, or when a loved one needs urgent medical help, it becomes difficult to detach ourselves, and stop our minds from thinking. Our loved one's are our responsibility, and in a crisis shouldn't we be thinking and worrying, and trying to solve our problems? Yoga says no, it is not necessary to think or to worry, while facing a crisis. It is important to remain calm and peaceful.

You will find that when you do not let external events disturb you, the external conditions of your life change by themselves for the better. The philosophy of non-dualism explains that there is only one energy that takes different forms. Whatever energy we give out comes back to us. When we are thinking or worrying, or experiencing any other negative emotions, we are only attracting more negative events into our lives. The fastest way to change an undesirable condition in our lives is not by thinking or worrying, it is by changing the negative energy that caused the condition. We do this by changing our emotions or what we are being. When we are being something positive like peaceful or happy, we attract events in our life that make us feel peaceful and happy. Therefore in the face of any problem, remain detached, and change what you are being to something positive. You will also discover that when you remain aware and peaceful, and stop the mind from thinking, you are able to access the great wisdom that you have within you. An idea or a thought will suddenly surface, which will help you solve your problem, or help you move forward in your life.

One must develop a sense of trust in the universe, process of life, or God (you may use any word to describe Ultimate Reality). God takes care of us and brings us all that we need. There is a very good reason why this happens. God is not separate from us. We are always a part of God, we are always a part of the Supreme Reality. Therefore, the Supreme Reality takes care of us. If we were separate, then we would have to fend for ourselves. When we are part of a Higher Reality, the Higher Reality takes care of us. This is an important point to remember when we are facing a crisis. Do not worry and do not fear. Trust. There will be highs and lows in life, but we are not alone in this process, and we have nothing to fear.

Detachment, and trust. These are two important words that one must understand. They can transform your life.

☙ 68 ❧

One should cast one's attention on the joy experienced, between the beginning and end of the sexual act. One will be completely filled with Energy, and through the bliss of love, one is united with God.

A common misconception today is that tantra is about sex. It isn't. Tantra is about liberation. The practices involving sex have frequently been misunderstood. They need to be seen for what they actually are – a spiritual practice intended to make one realize their True Self. Tantra believes that sex is meant for three purposes. For progeny, for pleasure, and for reaching God. Tantra was interested in using sex for reaching God. The sexual act is special in a particular way. The act of two individuals uniting into one is similar to the experience of the individual uniting with God.

Tantra was not against sensual pleasures. Tantrics believed that sensual pleasures should be enjoyed without attachment. The moment one becomes enslaved by them, one suffers. Sensual pleasures can enslave us. But they can also be used to liberate us. That is why in the original text of this verse, the words fire (vahni) and poison (visha) are used to refer respectively, to the beginning and to the end of the sexual act. What is poison for some, can for others be a means for liberation.

The tantric practices involving sex should be seen in proper light. They were not lewd activities for sensual pleasure. They are a method for liberation. The practices had rules and procedures to be followed. These practices were disclosed to very few people. The list of qualifications required to learn these practices was very long. People should not be attached to sensual pleasures. Otherwise, they would do these practices for sensual pleasure and not for achieving liberation. On the other hand, they could not be moralistic, and see these practices as lewd activities. The apirants who qualified for these practices were called *veera* or hero, because of their heroic attitude.

The master selected the right partner. Sometimes the master was a woman, a *yogini*. The man was not to be concerned about the beauty of his partner. He was to consider her not as a mere human being, but as a divine Goddess. What is remarkable about tantra is the respect given to women. Women were treated as equal to men. They were never considered to be inferior to men. In some tantric texts, the Goddess was elevated to a higher plane. In these texts, it was God (Shiva) that asked the questions, and the Goddess that gave the answers. In many ways, yoga and tantra were ahead of their time. Equality of women, realizing that we are one with God and each other, are concepts that the world is only now awakening to. The yogis and tantrics believed in them centuries ago.

Some of the practices involving sex had rituals of their own. In some instances, wine, fish and meat were consumed before the practice. The most well known of these practices was the *panchtattwa* (literally, five elements). Here the woman sits on the man's lap. The man enters her and the woman has her arms around his neck. The couple are supposed to synchronize their breath – breathe in and out at the same time. They look at each other's eyes and press their bodies together. The faces touch, the foreheads touch, and the eyes look directly at each other. They stay locked in that pose, breathing together, sometimes for hours.

For the purpose of this verse, it is not necessary to follow the practice described above. Any practice which gives joy or pleasure without harming anyone, is sufficient. Focus your attention on the joy experienced during the sexual act. Transform the sexual act into joy. Feel the love flowing. When there is enough love experienced, one dissolves, one's individual identity disappears. Then, there is only love. There is this incredible energy surging through one's body, after which, one is united with God. This energy is Kundalini. She starts her ascent up the spine, filling one with her ecstasy. That is what the verse means when it says, *One will be completely filled with Energy.*

The tantric sexual practices use the male-female duality, to transcend dualism. The male-female duality is the greatest duality in this world. This verse asks us to focus on the joy or love experienced during a sexual act. In unity, there is joy. When this joy or love is intense enough, one loses one's ego. That is what is beautiful about love. In love, oneness is felt – *through the bliss of love, one is united with God.*

☙ 69 ❧

At the time of sexual intercourse with a woman, there is great joy during an orgasm. That joy speaks of God's nature, and is of one's own self.

Verses 68 to 74 focus on the joy one experiences from the outside world. Not all these verses have to do with sex, but they are based on a single principle. When you experience joy from an external source, sometimes that joy is intense enough to cause an internal transformation. But in order for this to happen, one has to be aware of this joy. Awareness is important. Without awareness, no transformation can take place. The intensity of the joy causes the dormant energy, Kundalini, to rise. When that happens, one's True Self is revealed.

The joy of an orgasm is probably the most intense joy one can experience from the body. Yet it is only a fraction of the joy one experiences when one is united with God. The sages of India believed that the joy of liberation is millions of times more than the joy of an orgasm. Yet because of its intensity, the joy of an orgasm can lead us to God. What this verse is asking us to do is to be *aware* of the joy experienced during an orgasm. That joy may be sufficient to liberate us.

This verse and the previous verse is different from the teachings of yoga. Yoga generally teaches that one should avoid orgasms, as they are a waste of vital energy. Yogic practices also do not use sex as a means for enlightenment.

At the time of sexual intercourse with a woman. This practice can be done by women also. To make things simpler, some of the verses use a single gender. Tantra usually does not differentiate between men and women.

That joy speaks of God's nature, and is of one's own self. Joy is the basic nature of God. It is not only the joy of an orgasm that speaks of God's nature. Any joy experienced speaks of God's nature. However, the intensity of the joy experienced during an orgasm, gives an indication of the infinite joy of God. That joy *is of one's own self.* There is no separation between God and us. The joy of God's nature is also the joy of one's own self, because there is no difference between God and one's True Self. This joy is inherent in each and every one of us.

70

O Goddess, even in the absence of a woman – from the memory of the intense joy of the climax, while making love to a woman – one will experience a flood of joy.

Verse 70 is a variation of the previous verse. Even a woman is not necessary. Nor is having an actual orgasm necessary. Just the memory of it, the memory of the joy experienced is sufficient. If the memory is good, the intensity of the experience can be relived. It also goes to show that this joy is inherent in oneself. It is not dependent on external causes. Just using the memory is sufficient to draw this joy out.

one will experience a flood of joy. This refers to the point when one is liberated. The joy one experiences then, will be much greater than any joy one would previously have experienced.

All these verses lay stress on *being* joyful. And being aware of this joy. Joy and awareness is our true nature. Every time we are joyful and aware of being joyful, we take a step closer to God.

ೞ 71 ೞ

Whenever great joy is obtained, or when joy arises on seeing a friend or relative after a long time, one should meditate on that joy. Then the mind will be absorbed into joy.

Kashmir master Abhinavagupta in his book *Tantraloka*, calls the sense organs minor energy centers. Sometimes through the sense organs, one obtains joy or pleasure. Usually the pleasure obtained is not sufficiently intense to awaken the main center within. However, by focusing on that pleasure, by being aware of it, it is possible to trigger an internal reaction that awakens our main center, and liberates us.

Whenever great joy is obtained, or when joy arises on seeing a friend or relative after a long time, one should meditate on that joy. Whenever you experience a great amount of joy, be aware of it. When you suddenly see an old friend or relative after a long time, you immediately feel an abundance of joy. Usually we forget about the joy and concentrate on talking to our old friend. This verse says, forget the friend and concentrate on the joy; be aware of this joy. If there is no awareness of this joy, then this opportunity for liberation has been lost.

One does not meet an old friend or relative every day. Therefore, whenever one obtains joy, one should concentrate on it. The joy can be from any cause. These verses all emphasize what we are being. What we are doing is at the periphery. What we are being is at the center. Being something positive – happy, joyful, loving, can transform us. If we are being joyful, or happy, or loving for extended periods, we can be liberated.

Then the mind will be absorbed into joy. If we are being joyful, and we are aware of this joy, there will come a moment when we are liberated. At that moment, the mind will disappear. One will then feel an incredible amount of joy. This joy will be permanent. One will perpetually remain in a state of joy and awareness. Before liberation, we are aware or joyful for short periods of time. After liberation, we will permanently reside in this state. All that happens is that our true nature is uncovered through this process. Our true nature is joy. It is our mind that has prevented this joy from continuously being expressed. When there is no mind, our true nature flows out freely. It is like a dam that has been broken, and an abundance of water now flows out. In the same way, joy will be flowing freely from us into the world. A liberated person will sing, dance and love unconditionally. She is finally free, and has realized her true nature. All the happiness she was looking for, she has found within. The external world will no longer be required for finding joy, but for *expressing* her joy.

☙ 72 ❧

From the pleasure of eating and drinking, one experiences joy blossoming. One should become filled with that state of joy. Then great joy will be obtained.

The tantric sexual meditations are a part of a larger category of practices based on unity. Sometimes, when two objects unite (a man and a woman), joy is experienced. By focusing on that joy, one can be liberated. This is true of all sense organs and their objects. When our eyes see forms that are pleasing, joy is experienced. When our ears hear sounds that are pleasing, there is joy (Verse 73). When our mouth tastes food that is enjoyable, there is joy. That is what this verse is focusing on - on the pleasure obtained from eating or drinking something. This is a practice meant for those who love their food.

The beauty about tantra is that it accepts us fully without judgement, and seeks to improve us starting at the level where we are. It uses our personality to help us evolve and progress towards God. If we enjoy sex, we can use sex to increase our level of awareness. If we enjoy food or music, then it helps us use that to increase our awareness.

When eating or drinking something you enjoy, you find joy increasing or blossoming as the verse says. Focus on this joy, become full of this joy. Increase the joy you are feeling till you are simply radiating joy. Then a time will come when you will feel the immense joy of being united with God.

You will notice that the last few verses ask us to focus our attention back toward ourselves, to the joy we are feeling. An external factor may have caused the joy, but if we continue to concentrate on the external factor and not on the joy, then there will be no liberation. As the Katha Upanishad says, "God made the opening of the senses outwards. They go towards the world outside, not to the Self within. But a wise man who desired liberation, turned and looked inwards and found his Self." This is true of much of yoga. We are always extorted to redirect our attention back towards ourselves, to be aware of the self, and to look within. Even in these last few verses which are outward going, where joy is triggered from an external source, we are then asked to focus on the joy *we* are feeling - to redirect our attention back towards ourselves, and the joy we are feeling. Therefore, to be continuously aware of ourselves is always very important.

❧ 73 ❧

When one is enjoying singing and other pleasures of the senses, great joy arises. The yogi should become one with that joy. Then, one experiences growth of self.

Joy can be experienced through any sense organ. People enjoy different types of sensual pleasures. Some enjoy singing or listening to music. There are certain sounds that appeal instinctively to one. Music can make one peaceful and happy. Listen to music that makes you happy. Or focus on other pleasures that make you happy or joyful. Then, turn your attention to the joy you are experiencing. *The yogi should become one with that joy.* Blend with that joy. Unite with that joy. Feel yourself becoming one with that joy. The idea is to make you become joyful. Then you will just *be* joyful. The sense organs are acting as a catalyst or a trigger for you to feel joy and become joyful. The idea is to maintain that state of joy – *become one with joy.* You will find some people in life who remain happy, upbeat, even though they face circumstances in their life that are far from satisfactory. There are others who tend to brood over the negative aspects of their lives. This verse asks us to remain happy, to become one with joy. Then we are joyful, no matter what situation we are facing in life. Our reaction to every situation in life remains joyful. The Persian poet Rumi gave a wonderful definition of Sufism. He said that Sufism means to be joyful when disappointment comes. That is what this verse is also teaching us.

Then, one experiences growth of self. The small self, the ego disappears, replaced by God in human form. We are all God in human form. It is when our ego disappears that we experience the Divinity within us.

☙ 74 ❧

Wherever the mind finds satisfaction – in that very place focus one's attention. Then, the Supreme Bliss of one's true nature will manifest itself.

People find happiness, pleasure, joy, in different things. Meditations do not have to be sitting meditations. One may find peace or joy going for a walk in the morning, watching a sunset, looking at some beautiful mountains, holding a small baby in one's lap, laughing at anything. It is usually simple things that give us joy. Find out what works for you, what brings you happiness. It should not be something that hurts or harms any living being. Practice that activity. Then focus on the happiness you feel. The words "joy" and "happiness" can be used interchangeably in the last few verses. By remaining joyful, and being aware of this joy, one's true nature is revealed.

A larger point needs to be understood about Tantra. Tantra is not against pleasures of the senses. Tantra is not against money, sex, singing, dancing or any other sensual pleasures. Tantra believes life is to be enjoyed. If a person is not happy, then how can they give happiness to others? If a person has no money, then how can she give money to the needy or the poor? If a person has no joy, then how can she bring joy to others? Also, everything in life is a part of God – the good, the bad, the beautiful, the ugly. Therefore, it asks us to accept everything. If you reject anything, you reject a part of God. Enjoy everything, but without attachment. Do not be addicted or attached to any pleasure. Do not let your happiness depend on external pleasures. Enjoy pleasures while they last. If they are no longer there, move on and remain happy.

Tantra does not believe in repression or self-denial. Pleasures of the body are to be enjoyed and then transcended. Pleasures of the soul are much more enjoyable (there is infinitely more joy), than pleasures of the body. After enjoying pleasures of the body, you can move on to the higher pleasures of the soul. Yet, if you try and repress pleasures of the body, the desire for these pleasures will resurface later and inhibit your progress towards enlightenment. Sex is a natural bodily instinct. It was never meant to be denied. If you repress it, it will again surface later. That is why religions keep having problems with their monks. Scandals regarding sex keep arising from time to time. Tantra would say, let people enjoy sex. When they have had enough, they will seek higher pleasures.

There is a story in the life of Buddha that explains this. Buddha was born in a royal family. His father, the king, had been warned that his son would grow up to be a great spiritual master. His father tried everything to prevent this from happening. Buddha's childhood was one of abundance. He got everything he desired. There was no shortage of the pleasures of the senses, whether it was wine, good food, or fine clothes. Yet Buddha was not satisfied. He knew this could not be all there is to life. There had to be something more. His spiritual quest then became stronger, and he searched for the higher meaning of life. Therefore, it is not necessary to deny pleasures of the body. Once you experience them, you will realize that there is more to life than sensual pleasures. Then, your desire for spiritual progress will become stronger.

☙ 75 ❧

Concentrate on the state where sleep has not fully appeared, but the external world has disappeared. In that state, the Supreme Goddess is revealed.

There are four states of consciousness. Waking state (*jagrat*), dream state (*svapna*), deep sleep (*sushupti*), and full awareness (*turiya*). The dream state is also a state of sleep. It is a state of sleep, when we are sleeping and dreaming. The sleeping state has two categories – when we are dreaming (*svapna*), and when we are in deep sleep (*sushupti*). Turiya is the fourth state. It is a state of unbroken awareness and of enlightenment. Between the first two states, there is a gap or junction. There is a gap between the waking state and the sleeping state. It is in that gap that one will gain access to the fourth state of enlightenment.

This practice is focusing on the gap between the waking state and the sleeping state. It is a very subtle moment that passes quickly. *Concentrate on the state where sleep has not fully appeared, but the external world has disappeared.* You are not yet asleep, but the external world, the images, the thoughts have stopped. You have to be aware, conscious of that point. The problem is that if you concentrate too hard, you will be fully awake. Then you will be in the waking state. One has to able to drift towards sleep, but retain some semblance of awareness. Then suddenly in a flash, you will enter the fourth state of full awareness.

The state of deep sleep is very close to the state of *Samadhi* or union with God. The main difference is that during the sleeping state, there is no awareness. In the sleeping state, we are said to be One with God. The soul is once again free of the body. That is why sleep refreshes us. It is a state of unity with God. We revert to our original state. By trying to remain aware as we drift into sleep, we remain aware as we return to our original state. It is in that gap between the waking state and the sleeping state that we return to our original state. By being aware when this happens, we reach our original state with awareness. Then, we are in a state of enlightenment.

76

One should fix one's sight on the place where light from the sun, lamp, etc. forms different colors. There indeed, one's True Self will reveal itself.

Kashmir Shaivism has many practices that concentrate on the center. Center between two breaths, between two movements, between two thoughts, or the center between the waking state and sleeping state (previous verse). This verse concentrates on the center between two colors. Why is the center so important? The Kashmir master, Kshemaraja, used to say that it is in the center that you will find God. Our world is full of dualities. Usually it is a pair of opposites – high-low, male-female, inbreath-outbreath, etc. It is in the center between the two that one finds the unifying principle. It is in the center that dualities end, and one finds God.

We see objects only because of light. The light can be from any source – the sun, moon, lamp, etc. This light forms different colors. Light in its pure form includes all colors. Look at an object that has two or more colors. Focus on the meeting point of two colors. On the space or the area where two colors meet. Look at this point without blinking the eyes. If the eyes tire, close them for a while, then open them and continue with the practice.

A time will come when the colors momentarily disappear and light returns to its original state. At that moment, your mind and ego will disappear, and you will return to your original state. The use of colors and light in this meditation is interesting. Just as light includes all colors, God includes all the forms of the universe. Everything in the universe is part of God. When the separate colors disappear, our separate sense of existence (our ego), disappears. When the colors become one with light, we become one with God – we return to our true state.

☙ 77 ❧

From the yogic practices of Karankini, Krodhana, Bhairavi, Lelihana and Khecari Mudras, the Supreme Reality is revealed.

The term Mudra is usually translated as attitude. Mudras are physical postures or movements that bring about a change in attitude, usually a deepening of awareness. The practices mentioned in this verse are obscure. They were meant to be learnt from a master. These practices are also described in a text called *Cidgaganacandrika*. Given below is a brief description of the practices. However, they should be practiced only under the guidance of a master.

Karankini Mudra is the repose of death. Lie down as if dead. Imagine the whole body with all its organs being dissolved into consciousness. It is a practice whereby one has to spend long periods being immobile and quiet.

Krodhana Mudra is the attitude of anger. One has to assume a tight or tense posture, and keep the mouth open. From the open mouth, one has to imagine swallowing worldly objects and notions, dissolving them into their pure essence.

Bhairavi Mudra is a very powerful practice. It is mentioned again in Verse 113. One's gaze is fixed externally without blinking the eyes, and one's attention is turned within.

Lelihana Mudra is the attitude of licking. One imagines licking and consuming the entire differentiation found in the universe.

Khecari Mudra here is different from the Khecari mudra of hatha yoga, where the tongue is rolled upwards to touch the roof of the mouth. In this system, it refers to the state of Shiva. It is a state where one has reached full awareness or enlightenment.

78

Sit by placing one buttock on a soft seat, with no support for the hands and feet. By staying in that position, one will be filled with the understanding of the Supreme Reality.

When you first read this verse, you may wonder how sitting in such a funny (even ridiculous) posture, could help one achieve enlightenment. One has to sit in a soft seat on one buttock, with the other buttock and feet and hands suspended in mid air, without any support. The answer is actually very simple. To sit in such a posture requires a great deal of balance. One has to be fully aware, totally focused in the present, to maintain such a posture. If the mind starts wandering, you lose awareness of the present moment. Then, you lose your balance and you topple over. This meditation like all other meditations simply brings you to the present moment. By being in the present, you are in a state of awareness, where there are no thoughts. If you remain in a state of awareness for a long enough period, you will permanently reside in awareness, and achieve enlightenment.

Something similar happens with mountaineering. Mountain climbers are constantly at the risk of losing their lives. Inclement weather, a small slip, an avalanche, a falling rock striking them, and their lives are lost. They cannot let their mind wander to the past or to the future. It is too dangerous. They feel a great sense of peace while climbing. This peace actually comes from living in the present. By keeping the mind silent and remaining aware. Yet it is not necessary to do mountain climbing in order to feel this peace. To feel this peace, one simply has to be in the present, living life in awareness from moment to moment.

☙ 79 ❧

Sitting comfortably, curve the arms overhead, in the form of an arch. By absorbing the mind in the space of the armpits, Great Peace will come.

For the purpose of this meditation, one can sit in any position that makes one comfortable. One can even sit on a cushion. Then raise your arms above your head, and join your hands with the palms facing each other. The elbows should be bent so that the posture is comfortable. The arms and hands now form an arch above the head. Now close your eyes and focus your attention on the area of the armpits. Remain aware of the area of the armpits. That is what the verse means when it says, absorb the mind in the space of the armpits.

Certain postures increase our awareness of particular parts of the body. For example, if you bend forward and touch your toes, you immediately feel a stretching sensation in the legs. The posture described in this verse increases our awareness of the armpits. When you sit in this posture, you immediately *feel* the armpits. Then it becomes easier to focus your attention on the armpits. It is not necessary to look at the armpits. Just close your eyes and fix your awareness, your attention on the armpits. Normally when one's fixes one's attention on a particular part of the body, the mind may start wandering after a while. In this meditation, it is easier to maintain one's attention on the armpits. That is because in this posture one continuously *feels* the armpits. When we continuously maintain our awareness on a particular part of the body, the mind remains silent. A time comes when the mind becomes permanently silent. It is then that we experience Great Peace, as the verse says. This is a simple meditation that can be practiced by almost anyone.

☙ 80 ❧

Look firmly without blinking, at the gross form of any object. The mind will be without support, and within a short while one will reside in Shiva.

There are several "looking" techniques given in this text, which involve looking at something without blinking the eyes. Most looking techniques in yoga are called Trataka. They are very simple, powerful and direct methods of stilling the mind. There are a few rules about these techniques that need to be followed. The practices of Trataka are heat producing. They heat the body to a small extent. They should, therefore, not be practiced when one is feeling hot. They should be done in pleasant, comfortable surroundings. These practices should also be done without wearing glasses or contact lenses. In case you wear glasses, remove them and adjust the distance of the object you are looking at, so that you no longer have double vision.

Look firmly without blinking, at the gross form of any object. Choose an object you love. You will find it easier to concentrate on. It could be a symbol, a picture, an idol, candle flame, your nose tip, mandala, etc. Avoid looking directly at the sun or the moon. You may look at a rising or setting sun, or the reflection of the sun or moon in water. Once you choose an object, try not to change it. If you change it, your progress may be delayed.

The most important thing is to look firmly without blinking. Looking firmly means to look continuously. The movement of the eyes is somehow connected to the thought process. If you stop the eyes from moving, even blinking, all thoughts stop. When you do this, you may find the eyes becoming tired. In that case, close the eyes for a short period of time, then open them and resume the practice. Gradually the time you can keep the eyes open without blinking, will increase. Simultaneously, the time you spend without thinking also increases.

The mind will be without support, and within a short while one will reside in Shiva. Thoughts are like oxygen for the mind. The mind needs a continuous stream of thoughts in order to survive. If you stop thinking, the mind automatically dies out. It becomes still, silent. It loses its independence and finally comes under your control. When you look at something without blinking, you automatically stop thinking. If you do this long enough, the mind permanently becomes silent. The time taken for all this to happen is not very long. For most people, it may not be more than a few minutes. If the mind is silent for a few minutes without any thoughts, it permanently becomes silent. That is why these looking techniques are so powerful. They produce results in a very short span of time.

one will reside in Shiva. One will reside in God. One will reside in one's natural state. When the mind falls silent, we revert to our original state. A state of full awareness, filled with immense joy.

☙ 81 ❧

With mouth wide open, throw the tongue upwards to the center of the palate. Fix attention on the middle of the tongue, and feel the sound Ha being uttered there. Then, one will be dissolved in Peace.

For this practice, keep the mouth open. It should not be so wide open that one becomes uncomfortable. Now lift the tongue upwards and backwards, so that it touches the roof of the mouth, the palate. Place your awareness on the middle of the tongue and feel the sound *ha* being uttered there. The sound *ha*, is the sound of a particular Sanskrit alphabet. It is pronounced more like *hh*. In this posture, you will feel this sound when you breathe in and you will feel this sound when you breathe out. After a while, the tongue may feel tired. You should lower the tongue for a short period, and then raise it again and resume the practice. The sound *hh* is not a sound that is to be uttered out aloud. It is a sound that is to be felt. It is a natural sound – it is the sound of your breath.

Listening to the sound of one's own breath is a very important meditation. It is a natural way of focusing and stilling the mind. The practice of listening to one's breath is dealt with later in the text. The meditation given in this verse is a variation of that practice. Normally our inbreath makes a particular sound and our outbreath makes a different sound. In this particular meditation, because the mouth is open and the tongue is raised to touch the palate, the sound *hh* is heard with the inbreath as well as the outbreath.

The breath is the most natural rhythm of the body. It continues spontaneously throughout our life. Focusing on the sound of our breath immediately calms our mind. It is a natural rhythm, which the mind is attracted to, and easily absorbed in. When you practice this meditation, you will find yourself becoming calm and peaceful very quickly. If you are ever tense or upset or angry in your life, listen to the sound of your breath. It will have an immediate calming effect on you.

It is possible to be aware of the sound of the breath for long periods of time, without any thought disturbing you. If you find it difficult to remain aware during any other meditation (thoughts keep disturbing you), try the practice given in this verse. Or better still, just listen to the sound of your breath (described in Verses 154-156). You will not be disappointed with the progress you achieve.

ଓ 82 ଛ

Seated on a bed or couch, continuously imagine one's own body to be without support. The instant the mind disappears, one's fixed place of residence disappears.

It is important to understand that we are not our body. We think that we are the body, and that is the cause of our suffering and our bondage. Some of the earlier verses gave meditations to break our attachment with the body. This verse is somewhat similar. One should sit on a bed or couch in a comfortable posture. Then continuously imagine one's own body to be without support. That means, imagine your body, your self to be weightless. In truth, we are weightless and without support. Our soul has no weight. It is the body that has weight, and we are not the body. It is the body that limits us and binds us to the ground. Here, we are trying to break the limitations of the body, by imagining our body to be weightless.

There are many verses in this text that deal with changing our beliefs, or imagining something, like our body to be weightless. To some people what we are imagining may seem difficult or even far-fetched. Yet they are not far-fetched. They have been reports of some yogis who have levitated during their meditation. They have defied the laws of gravity. Not only have they made their body weightless, they have actually lifted their body from the ground. Therefore, what this verse is asking us to imagine is not so far-fetched. This verse is basically giving us a method for detaching ourselves from the body. Sometimes we find it difficult to detach ourselves from the body or believe that we are not the body, because we continuously feel the *weight* of the body. We are constantly reminded of the body, because the body binds us to the ground or to a seat. This practice attempts to break that limitation by asking one to imagine that one's body is weightless.

The instant the mind disappears, one's fixed place of residence disappears. The moment the mind disappears, one is liberated. Then, although one is in the body, one no longer identifies with the body. One's attachment to the body is broken. One no longer believes they are the body. The body is now only a vehicle to experience life. A liberated person is one with God. As God exists everywhere, she now also exists everywhere. That is what the verse means, when it says that one's fixed place of residence disappears. For most people, their fixed place of residence is the body. A liberated person has outgrown the body. She is one with God, and feels one with everything else.

83

O Goddess, by experiencing the rhythmic movement of the body in a moving vehicle, or in a still place by swinging the body slowly. Then the mind becomes calm, and one obtains a flood of divinity.

The mind is attracted to rhythms. Rhythms hold the mind's attention for long periods of time. That is why being aware of the breath is such an important practice. The breath is the natural rhythm of the body. Rhythms are found elsewhere in life. Most people enjoy listening to some form of music. There are some rhythmic beats or sounds that appeal to us instantly. These sounds make us happy or calm, and bring our attention to the present. When we listen to music we enjoy, we forget our problems, and focus our attention on the present moment, on the sound that we are enjoying.

This meditation is doing something similar. It is using a rhythm to calm the mind. It uses the rhythm of the movement of the body. One has to be aware of the rhythmic movement of the body in a moving vehicle. It is important to understand the context and time period in which these verses were written. These verses were written centuries ago. A vehicle in those days meant a bullock cart "driven" by one or two cows. Today, a vehicle usually means a car. If you are driving a car today in a modern expressway, you will feel no movement or rhythmic movement of the body. Yet if you were sitting in a bullock cart pulled by a cow, in a broken down road in ancient India, your body would be moving in a rhythmic manner. It would sway back and forth. You experience something similar when you ride a horse. As the horse moves, your body moves. Focus your attention on the rhythmic movement of the body. As the mind is attracted to rhythms, it is easier to focus and hold your attention on the rhythmic movement of the body. The longer you hold your attention, the longer you remain in the present moment, in a state of awareness, without any thoughts. And that is what this meditation is trying to do. It uses the rhythmic movement of the body to calm the mind, and bring it to the present.

or in a still place by swinging the body slowly. In a still place, swing your body slowly in circles. It is not necessary to use a horse or vehicle to experience the rhythmic movement of the body. In a still place, move the body slowly in circles, or rock the body to and fro. There are many ways to move the body in a rhythmic manner. Some people enjoy dancing. This meditation can even be practiced then. Whenever you are moving your body rhythmically, concentrate on the rhythmic movement of the body.

Then the mind becomes calm, and one obtains a flood of divinity. A rhythmic movement calms the mind. The mind is easily absorbed in a rhythmic movement. The mind stops thinking. It becomes peaceful. It is only aware of the movement of the body. Young babies are put to sleep by gently rocking them. When babies are agitated, or start crying, their mother usually picks them up and pats them gently, or moves them to and fro to calm them. Rhythmic movement of the body calms the mind. This is a natural phenomena. This meditation uses a natural phenomena to still the mind.

84

Look continuously at a clear sky, without moving oneself. From that moment O Goddess, one will obtain the form of God.

Our true nature is infinity. We are one with God, who is infinite. It is our identification with our ego, or our mind and body, that limits us. This meditation tries to break the limitations imposed by the mind and the body. It does this by looking at something infinite. It is similar to Verse 60, where one has to look at a vast open space, with no mountains, trees, walls, etc. This is easier to practice because it is difficult to find a vast open place with no trees or mountains. It is easier to find a clear sky with no clouds.

It is best to practice this meditation lying down, looking up at the sky. *Look continuously.* This is also a looking technique. Like all looking techniques, is should be done without blinking or moving the eyes. When we stop the movement of the eyes, we stop all thoughts. This by itself is sufficient for enlightenment. Yet this meditation works at two other levels.

at a clear sky. This is important. A clear blue sky gives a sense of infinity. If there are clouds, then something finite, something with a boundary has come into the picture. The sense of infinity is lost. When you are looking at a pure blue sky, you are looking at something infinite. The mind cannot coexist with infinity. The longer you look at something infinite, the weaker the mind becomes. Ultimately, the mind disappears altogether.

Looking at something infinite is important for another reason also. We need another object by which to define ourselves by. We cannot exist in a vacuum. Our sense of separateness, our individual identity is obtained in relation to something else. We see a bird, a table, mountains, trees, a house, another human being, and we define ourselves as being different from that. We (the subject) see ourselves as separate and different from that particular object. When we look at a clear sky, there is no object there by which we can compare and define ourselves. (That is also why a clear sky is important. When there are clouds, there is a definable object that we can compare ourselves to). When there is no object, there is also no subject. Our ego collapses. Our separate identity disappears. We become one with the Whole. In Verse 33, and in Zen Buddhism, one practices a similar technique. A person is asked to sit in front of a plain white wall. That person has to look at the wall continuously. The effect is the same. There is no object in the wall by which one can define oneself. There is nothing separate from us because there is nothing else. When there is nothing separate, we no longer remain separate. We become one with God.

without moving oneself. In all looking meditations, one should not move the body. In looking meditations, one is stopping the eyes from moving, or even blinking. When the body moves, the eyes automatically move, and the effect of the meditation is lost.

From that moment O Goddess, one will obtain the form of God. Results are achieved in this meditation very quickly. That is because three factors are working here – it is a looking technique, and by not moving the eyes, all thoughts stop. By looking at something infinite, we become infinite. And by not having an object to look at, our ego, our separate identity, disappears.

☙ 85 ❧

One should meditate that the entire space or sky, is absorbed in one's head. By absorbing the qualities of God, one will acquire the brilliant form of God.

Space has several qualities, similar to God. Just like God, space is eternal, supportless, all pervasive and silent. Space is supportless. Unlike physical objects which need a support, space requires no support. Space also exists everywhere. There is no place in this world where you cannot find space. Space is also silent. It is often said that you find God in the silence. In this meditation, one has to imagine that the entire space in this world is absorbed in one's head.

By absorbing space, you are absorbing the qualities of space. These are the same as the qualities of God, and also the same as your true nature. By absorbing these qualities, one *becomes* these qualities. That is, one becomes eternal, supportless and all pervasive. This is a meditation that changes our belief about ourselves. We believe we are the body or the mind, and that is why we do not see our real nature. Now we are asked to consider something else. That we are eternal, supportless, and all pervasive.

To practice this meditation, imagine all space being absorbed in your head. Continue to imagine space being absorbed in your head, till your head is nothing but space. Ultimately, you may get the feeling of headlessness. That you have no head, but only space. When this happens, you will be aware. Mystics have frequently described this feeling of headlessness. It is a state when the mind has fallen silent. Although one is still in the body, one no longer feels that one is the body. Instead, they feel a sense of unity with all of existence.

☙ 86 ❧

In the waking state there is some knowledge born of duality. In the dream state there are impressions of the exterior. In deep sleep there is complete darkness. Know all these states of consciousness to be the form of God. Then, one will be filled with the infinite light of God.

This is one of the few obscure verses in the text. The meditation is given in an indirect way. It is the same meditation that is given in the Mandukya Upanishad.

There are four states of consciousness. First, there is the normal waking state. Then there is the dream state. This is a state when we are sleeping, and also dreaming. The third state is the state of deep sleep, when there are no dreams. In this state, there is no duality. There is only darkness or void. This state is very close to the state of enlightenment. The difference is that in the dreamless sleep state, there is no awareness. The fourth state is the state of turiya, or superconsciousness. This fourth state is the state of enlightenment.

AUM is a very important syllable or sound. The Mandukya Upanishad teaches us that the A is supposed to stand for the waking state. The U stands for the dream state. The M stands for the deep sleep state. When A, U and M are sounded together as in AUM, then that sound represents the fourth state of consciousness. It is the highest state. It is the state of non-dualism and of love. It is the state of God.

The sound AUM has always been considered important. It is supposed to represent God and lead to God. The Katha Upanishad also says that this syllable AUM is indeed God. That those who know this sound get all that they desire.

Know all these states of consciousness to be the form of God. A, U, and M, which represent the different states of consciousness, should be sounded together as in AUM. That is the meaning of this sentence.

Use AUM for meditation. That is what this verse is teaching. AUM will lead us to God. How does one use AUM in a meditation practice? The most common way is to chant AUM. The correct way to chant AUM is given in the commentary to verse 39. Breathe in and while breathing out, open your mouth and make the sound aaa. Then, start closing your mouth. When your mouth is semi-closed, the aaa sound becomes uuu. When the mouth is fully closed, the uuu sound becomes mmm. When you complete this practice (or even while doing this practice), you will notice a definite change in yourself. You will become more calm, more peaceful. You will feel refreshed. You mind will quieten down.

There are certain words, certain sounds and mantras that have the power to transform us. Some of these sounds were discovered by the ancient sages, when they were deep in meditation. One does not know exactly how they work. Many of the mantras do not have any meaning. But these sacred sounds have the power to change us. Of all the sacred sounds and mantras, there is none higher than AUM. Chanting AUM is a very effective way to still the mind.

≈ 87 ≈

Similarly, on a completely dark night during the dark half of the lunar month, concentrate for a long time on the darkness. One will then be propelled towards the form of God.

In complete darkness, forms are not visible. To see objects, light is needed. With the help of light, one can see the form, shape and boundary of an object. In darkness, nothing is visible. There is just darkness.

The meditation given here is similar to Verse 84, where one had to continuously look at a clear sky. Here, on a completely dark night, we look at the darkness. It is like looking at a black wall. To transcend the world of form and duality that we are used to, we continuously look at a place that has no forms or objects. Our sense of self, our sense of separate identity, is dependent on other objects being present. When other objects are present, we see ourselves as different from those objects. Yet, what we are seeing is an illusion. It is an illusion of separateness. We see ourselves as being separate from other people. How do we break this illusion and see true reality? One of the ways is by looking at a place where no other forms or objects are visible. When we see nothing apart from us, we no longer remain apart. We become a part of God.

One has to practice this on a completely dark night, where there is no light from the moon. When you practice this, you may experience visions or images appearing. These images are just the release of one's suppressed feelings or fears. One should not be disturbed by these images. Instead, one should continue with the practice.

One will then be propelled towards the form of God. When one cannot see any other object, one's ego collapses. In order to exist, one's ego needs other objects. Just as the mind needs thoughts to survive, the ego needs other objects. Without the support of other objects, the ego collapses. Then, one rapidly moves towards God.

☙ 88 ❧

Similarly, in the absence of a dark night, close the eyes and concentrate on the darkness in front of one. Opening the eyes, see the dark form of God spreading everywhere. One will then become one with God.

This practice is a variation of the previous one. It is not always possible to find a completely dark night, especially if you live in a city. There will always be light somewhere that will make it difficult to practice the previous meditation.

The meditation given in this verse is not fully dependent on external circumstances. However, it is better to practice this meditation in a room that is partially or completely dark. Close your eyes and concentrate on the darkness in front of you. Keep looking at the darkness, till one is completely absorbed in darkness. Then open your eyes and see darkness spreading everywhere. When you first open your eyes, you may see certain objects. Try and see everything being enveloped by darkness. After a while, there is only darkness. Now, no objects can be seen in the external world. It is then that one will become one with God.

The dark form of God the verse refers to is darkness. When the eyes are opened, one has to see this darkness spreading everywhere. If you see darkness spreading everywhere, then you have reached a state of enlightenment. After a while, the darkness will disappear, and you will see objects the way you normally do. However, now you will permanently reside in a state of enlightenment. In case after opening your eyes, you do not see darkness spreading everywhere, then you will have to continue with this practice everyday, till you are successful.

People are more used to hearing about meditation practices using light. Practices involving darkness are rare. However, light and darkness are not opposites. They are different degrees of the *same thing*. Both can be used to enter the Divine.

☙ 89 ❧

When any sense organ is obstructed externally or is restrained by one, from carrying out its function – one will then enter the void that is beyond duality. There indeed, one's True Self will be revealed.

Our senses are outward going. They do not go within. But God is found within. When you block any sense organ, consciousness is redirected inwards. Your awareness is no longer outwards. It is now focused within. It is within that there is no duality. It is within that you find God.

When you look with your eyes, you see various forms and objects in the external world. When you close your eyes, you see only darkness. There are no forms, no objects, no dualities (two or more separate objects). There is only darkness, there is only unity. Similarly, with your ears you hear the various sounds of the world. When you close your ears, there is only silence. There are no dualities, no varied sounds. There is only one thing, and that is silence. There is nothing apart from silence. Therefore within, you will not find two (dualism), or more. Neither two sounds, nor two objects. You will find only One. When the eyes are closed there is only darkness, when the ears are closed, there is only silence.

These examples can be extended to other sense organs. Through the nose, we smell different smells. When the nose is closed, we smell nothing. There is void, nothing. Similarly, through the mouth we taste different foods, or speak different words. When the mouth is closed, we taste and say nothing. There is only void.

The example of waves on an ocean is used to explain all this. On the surface of an ocean, there are lots of waves. However, deep down there is only the ocean. There are no waves, no separate forms. It is the same with human beings. Through our sense organs, we see, hear, taste, touch and smell lots of different things. However, within there is no diversity (dualism). There is only one thing and that is God. One can also say that within there is nothing, there is void or emptiness. Both mean the same. The important thing to understand is that it is within that one transcends dualism. It is within that one sees the ocean and not the waves. It is within that we see ourselves as a part of God, and not as separate beings.

How does one practice this meditation? Sit comfortably and close any sense organ. It is preferable to do this with the eyes or ears. Do not close the nose, as you will not be able to breathe. The mouth in any case will be closed when you are practicing a sitting meditation. If you are closing your eyes, then concentrate on the darkness you see within. If you are closing your ears, close your eyes as well and concentrate on the silence. When you stop any sense organ from carrying out its function, your awareness will be directed within. In this case, it will either be on the darkness or the silence experienced within.

꧁ 90 ꧂

Continuously recite the vowel A, without the sound M or H. Then O Goddess, a great flood of knowledge of God rises forcefully.

The sound of the vowel *a* in Sanskrit is like the sound of *a* in <u>a</u>merica. In this practice, *a* should be continuously chanted out loud, or silently in the mind. If you are chanting *a* mentally, you can continuously chant it. If you chant it out loud, then it can be chanted while breathing out. Breathe in and while breathing out, chant *aaaa*... When the breath is fully exhaled, breathe in again, and while breathing out, continue to chant the vowel *a*.

What is the significance of the vowel *a*? Why is it used for this practice? In Kashmir Shaivism, there is a Theory of the Alphabet. In that theory, *a* represents the consciousness of God. Chanting *a* increases our level of awareness. Ultimately, we reach a state of full awareness.

꧁ 91 ꧂

Make the sound H and concentrate on the end of the sound. As the mind will be without support, one will permanently touch God.

The sound *h* is the *visarga*, an alphabet in Sanskrit symbolized by the two dots of a colon. It is not a full *h* sound, it is more like a half *h* sound. The *h* is slightly suppressed.

This sound should also be made while breathing out. Make the sound *h* as you breathe out. Then breathe in again and make the sound *h* as you breathe out. The sound can be chanted out loud or said in the mind. Concentrate on the end of the sound. The sound *h* is a subtle sound that ends suddenly. It requires a higher level of awareness to notice it. Concentrating on the end of this sound immediately increases our level of awareness.

As the mind will be without support, one will permanently touch God. This meditation is similar to the previous one. Chanting a sound stops the mind from thinking. Particularly a sound like *h*, which requires a higher level of awareness to notice its end.

This meditation and the previous one have many practical benefits. They can be practiced when one is tense or angry. They immediately calm you down. You may face a situation in life, which makes you very tense or angry. You may have had a minor car accident, which was not your fault. Someone may have spoken to you and been very rude to you. You keep thinking about these events, sometimes hours after they have occurred. Your mind keeps racing away, and your blood pressure keeps rising. In these circumstances, the best way to calm yourself down is to chant a sound. It immediately stops your mind from thinking. When your mind stops thinking, you automatically become peaceful. Take a deep breath in and while breathing out, chant either *h* or *aaa* . . . There is a similar breathing technique in yoga called Bhramari, where instead of *h* or *a*, one make a continuous humming sound (like a bee), while breathing out. That too can be used in these situations.

In these tense situations, the mind races out of control. When you chant a sound, you instantly block out the mind. The mind stops thinking, and you become calm.

☙ 92 ❧

Meditate on one's own self in the form of space (or the sky), unlimited in all directions. Then, one will see one's own form as the unsupported energy of consciousness.

Our true nature is infinite. As we are a part of God, our true nature is that of God. God is not confined to a particular place. God exists everywhere, unlimited in all directions. God is infinite and so are we. We believe that we are the body. That we are confined to a particular place, called our body. But that is not the truth. That is an illusion. The body is a part of our ego, our sense of separate identity. To reach God, we have to destroy our ego. This verse shows us how to do that.

As long as we believe we are the body, our sense of self is limited to something very small. The verse asks us to believe that we are endless, like the sky, unlimited in all directions. In effect, we are changing our belief about ourselves. And that can be very powerful. When we change our belief, we change our reality. Our beliefs create our reality. There are people who believe that the world is a wicked, dangerous place. These people will find themselves experiencing just that. Events that occur in their lives will prove their belief – that the world is a dangerous place. There are other people who believe that making money is very difficult. These people will struggle all their lives to make money, thereby proving their belief about money. Therefore, we should be very careful about what we believe. To change our life for the better, we have to change our beliefs. New beliefs have a direct, immediate impact on our lives.

This verse is giving us a new belief that can liberate us. Believe that you are endless space, infinite, unlimited in all directions. This meditation can also be practiced as a sitting meditation, with eyes closed. Imagine that you are not the body, but something infinite, like space, existing everywhere.

When we believe we are infinite, we stop believing we are the body. And that has a profound and immediate impact on our lives. We stop worrying and thinking too much, because most of our worrying and thinking is about *the body*. What the body needs. What pleasures the body desires. When we realize we are not the body, we no longer care whether our desires are fulfilled or not. If we do not acquire enough money to give the body the pleasures it desires, it does not matter. Even if the body is facing death, it does not matter. We are not the body, and we will survive, even when the body is destroyed.

When we believe we are not the body, we immediately become calm. We become detached from the external world. External events only affect the body. They do not affect us (our Real Self). They can have no impact on us. When we can detach ourselves from the external world, our mind becomes still. It is no longer troubled by the external world. When the mind falls silent, we become free.

If we are not the body, then what are we? The answer is given in the second part of the verse. We are consciousness. When you understand you are not the body, you realize you are awareness, the One who is aware, of all the events unfolding in your life. Consciousness, our Real Self, is eternal. It is unaffected by all the events of our life, and can never be destroyed.

When you practice this verse, you reach a stage when you suddenly detach from your body. Your body is still there, it does not decay or die, but you no longer identify with it. You at last realize the truth about your body – that it is nothing substantial, it is empty, void. You instead experience this infinite expanse of space, this ocean of awareness, that includes everything. You feel one with this space, and you realize that everything in this universe is one with this space. You experience the greatest truth in the world, that there is only One Being. Your sense of self is no longer the body. It has now grown to something infinite. And as the Brihad-aranyaka Upanishad wonderfully puts it – the Seer is alone and there is no other.

ও 93 ঌ

Pierce any part of your body with a sharp needle, point, etc. Then join your awareness to that very place. There, you will obtain the purity of God.

When you pierce any part of your body, you experience pain. You then have to focus your awareness on that very place. That place is the source of the pain. This practice is unusual in that it uses pain. In fact, any body sensation can be used. There may be a part of your body that is feeling stiff. You can focus your awareness on that very part.

This practice uses pain to focus the mind. When you are experiencing pain in any part of the body, it is difficult not to be aware of it. Conversely, it is easy to concentrate on because it is such a strong sensation. When you are able to maintain your awareness for prolonged periods, the mind falls silent and one is liberated.

This is not a practice recommended for everyone. Piercing the body on a regular basis is not recommended. If it has to be done, a part of the body should be used, that cannot be damaged. One such place can be the lower part of the ear, which is normally pierced in women for wearing earrings. This meditation can also be practiced by those who are experiencing pain due to some other factor. They may be suffering from arthritis, or recovering from an operation.

Pain can also help liberate us by forcing us to accept our life situation. Sometimes the pain we experience in our lives is so strong, so unavoidable, that we have no choice but to accept it. This is true not just of physical pain but also of emotional pain. There are times when life completely overwhelms us. Things go wrong and we feel we are unable to cope. The magnitude of events is such that one feels that one is no longer in control of one's life, and that there is nothing we can do to immediately change our external life situation for the better. In that moment of helplessness, one suddenly gives up – one surrenders. We suddenly accept our life situation, because we feel too overwhelmed to keep resisting it. It is in that surrender, that total acceptance that our ego suddenly disappears. There is no more resisting life, no more fighting with life, just complete acceptance and surrender. In that moment our ego collapses, and we are immediately filled with bliss. We are then grateful to our life situation for helping us reach a state of enlightenment. There are stories of prisoners awaiting execution, who have surrendered and have experienced the bliss of liberation. There was nothing they could do to change their external life situation. They then completely accepted life, and obtained the bliss of enlightenment. Sometimes, in the darkest moments of our lives, we are very close to liberation.

ଓ 94 ଌ

One should meditate like this – "There is nothing inside me. No mind, intellect, bones, organs, etc." By this meditation one will abandon all thoughts. By being in a state without thoughts, one will reach God.

Some of the earlier meditations had asked us to consider our body, or parts of our body to be empty. This is a variation of those practices. In this meditation, we have to consider that there is nothing inside the body. No mind, intellect, bones, organs, or anything else.

This meditation can be practiced as a sitting meditation. Sit comfortably and close your eyes. Now imagine that there is nothing inside your body. Your body is just an empty shell, with the skin as the outer covering. Also imagine that the body has no reasoning facility. There is no mind, no thoughts, no intellect. There is nothing. When everything is discarded from your body, you are left with awareness. You are simply aware.

One can also practice this meditation throughout the day. Continuously believe that you have nothing inside your body. No mind, no organs, nothing. This is similar to a practice suggested by mystics, such as Rumi and Harding. They said, believe that you are headless. That you have no head. Here, we have to believe not only that we have no mind, but also nothing else inside our body.

By this meditation one will abandon all thoughts. By being in a state without thoughts, one will reach God. By imagining we have no mind, we stop our thought processes. When there is no mind, there can be no thoughts. When we remain without thoughts, we reach God.

95

Remain firm in one's understanding that a small part of anything, with a name, is a tempting illusion. Thus, the primary quality of one's true nature is unity. From this understanding one will not remain separate any longer.

Anything that has a form or a name is an illusion. What is the illusion? The illusion is that the form has a separate self. When we see an object, whether it is inanimate or living, we imagine it to have a separate identity. That is why we even give it a name. The name signifies its separate existence, its separate identity. In truth, all objects are empty. They are empty of a separate self. They have no separate self, but are full of God.

If we believe that we have a separate existence, fear comes into our lives. We then believe that we have a beginning and an end. That at some stage we will die, and become nothing. Something can never become nothing. Nor can something come from nothing. The truth is that we never die, we only change form. We always see evidence of this in nature. A cloud turns into rain. Rain water enters fruits and vegetables, and later becomes a part of the human body. Or it becomes a part of the river, and flows into the sea.

This verse is telling us that no object or form of any kind has an independent self. Everything is part of the Whole, everything is a part of God. Our primary quality is unity. We are one with God and everything else in this universe. When you know this, fear leaves your life. You realize that you can never be destroyed. Ultimately, nothing can harm you.

The way to practice this meditation is to change what you believe. Believe that what you are seeing is an illusion. That you or any other object has no separate self. Everything is God. The verse says that one has to remain firm in one's understanding. This means that one should continuously believe that one has no separate self. Our sense of separate self is our ego. When we believe that we have no separate self, our ego starts dissolving. It is only a matter of time before our belief turns into reality.

This verse, like the previous one, attempts to dissolve our ego. When we believe that we have a separate self, our true nature remains hidden. When our outer covering, our ego, is peeled away, then our true nature appears. What does it feel like, when our ego is dissolved? The Brihad-aranyaka

Upanishad puts it beautifully, when it says, "Where there seems to be another, there one may see another, one may touch another and one may know another. But when one becomes clear like water, the Seer is alone and there is no other."

☙ 96 ❧

When one sees a desire having risen, one should immediately end it. One will then be absorbed in the very place from which the desire arose.

A desire can be an urge, or a thought, or a feeling. Basically, all desires are a form of energy. Energy that is flowing, energy that has been increased. The verse says that the moment one observes a desire having arisen, one should *immediately* end it. When you immediately end a desire, or suddenly stop it, this energy that has arisen has to go somewhere. It has no choice, but to return to its Source. All energy comes from God. When you suddenly stop a desire, this energy has to return to God. As it returns to God, it takes you with it. *One will then be absorbed in the very place from which the desire arose.*

The emphasis is on immediately ending a desire. When you suddenly end a desire, you block it with greater force. That is when this energy rushes back to its source. When you end a desire, you must remain aware. That is how you will return with this energy to God. If you end a desire and start thinking again, then the energy of the desire will be changed to the energy of your new thoughts. Energy then, will no longer go back to its source. It will only take on new forms.

☙ 97 ❧

When desire or knowledge have not arisen in me – who am I?, in that condition. That is truly my essential Reality. By reflecting in this way, one will be absorbed into that Reality.

Who am I before desire or knowledge have arisen? This is a very direct inquiry that liberates us. It is a method that was made famous by Ramana Maharshi, the Indian saint of the 20th Century. Maharshi's method was a shorter version of this verse. He used to say that one should always inquire, "Who am I?" Even when you have a thought, ask yourself this question. "To whom do these thoughts belong. Who is this I?" This is a method that requires no strenuous physical activity, or chanting or meditation. It is a direct inquiry that dissolves our ego. Who am I really at the core of my Being? This question removes all our layers of conditioning, and takes us to our true nature.

When desire or knowledge have not arisen in me – who am I?, in that condition. The verse asks a slightly different question. Who am I before desire or knowledge have arisen? Desire and knowledge arise when there is an ego. Without an ego, there can be no desire. In our highest state there is only One, therefore how can there be any desire? For desire to exist, there must be objects separate from us that we can desire. In our highest state there is nothing separate from us and therefore there is no desire. When the ego arises, we feel separate from other objects in this world, and the desire to acquire some of them arises. It is the same with knowledge. It is our ego that has knowledge, limited knowledge on various subjects. The verse goes on to say that the state we are in before desire or knowledge have arisen, is our true state. It is our original, pure state. By reflecting in this manner, by asking yourself this question, you will be lead into that original state.

To reach our true state, which is before thoughts or desires arise, we first have to look at the source of our thoughts or desires. When a thought or desire arises, ask yourself this question – Who am I? To whom do these thoughts belong? When you do this, your awareness is directed back towards yourself. Who is this small I, this entity, to whom these thoughts belong? You will realize that there is no such entity. The mind cannot survive when the light of awareness is turned on it. The mind is nothing but a bundle of thoughts. When you direct your attention back towards yourself, searching for the source of your thoughts, you will find that your mind automatically falls silent. The source of our thoughts, our mind, is a shallow entity. It has no separate existence. When you become self-aware, this false entity disappears. It is nowhere to be found. There is only awareness and silence. You will then discover that our true state is awareness. Awareness is our essential reality, before thoughts or desires arise.

This meditation has many wonderful, practical implications. Sometimes, we experience fear, self-doubt, or an addictive desire. The next time this happens to you, ask yourself these questions – To whom do these fears belong to? Or to whom do these doubts or desires belong to? As you peer within, you will find that there is no such entity. Then, all your fears and doubts will be washed away, and you will rest in awareness.

ଓଃ 98 ଛ

When desire or knowledge have arisen, one should stop reflecting on them, and consider the Self as identical with consciousness. Then, one's true nature appears.

When desire or knowledge arise, our ego gets strengthened. When we have a desire, we think – I want this or I want that. With knowledge it is similar – I know this, or I know that. This "I" is the ego. Where the "I" is strong, we are bound. When there is no "I", we are free. That is why this verse asks us to stop reflecting on desire or knowledge. You are only reinforcing your ego, or your small "I". Instead, believe that you are consciousness. That your Real Self is consciousness. You will then become a witness. This is also the answer to the question raised in the previous verse. Who am I before desire or knowledge have arisen? I am consciousness. In the previous verse, one finds the answer by looking for the source of our thoughts, and realizing that there is no separate entity, there is only awareness. In this meditation, we simply stop thinking about our desires, and return to being aware. The process in these two verses is a little different, but the end result is the same – one returns to a state of awareness.

To practice this verse, every time a desire arises, stop thinking about it. Instead, believe you are awareness. Return to being aware, and living in the present moment. When you do this, your ego will get weaker and your level of awareness will get stronger. Ultimately your ego will disappear, and you will reside in awareness.

This verse is not for suppression of desires or expression of desires. It seeks to encourage awareness or witnessing. Don't identify with the "I" of the desire. That I must do this or I must achieve that. That only strengthens the ego. Instead practice witnessing. If a desire arises, observe it, and let it pass.

ര 99 ഇ

The true nature of God is without cause and without support. Any person's knowledge or perception is not this. O Dear One, in this way, one becomes Shiva.

God is unconditional. That is the meaning of this verse. This is an important point to understand. It is a truth that can transform our lives.

God's existence is forever. God's existence does not depend on any cause or support. God has no beginning, no end. More importantly, God's nature is without cause or support. This means that God's nature remains the same. It does not depend on any cause or condition. Religions teach us of a God that is sometimes angry and sometimes loving. If we are nice, we are let into heaven. If we are not, we face the wrath of God, and go to hell forever. This verse says that all this is untrue. God's nature, God's love is unconditional. God's love is not dependent on any cause or condition. God loves us all the same whether we behave or misbehave. We sometimes believe that through our actions we can make God unhappy or angry. Nothing makes God unhappy or angry. God's nature is not dependent on any cause or condition. God's happiness or love needs no condition to exist. God's love is unconditional and freely given, and that is God's greatest gift to us. In turn, the greatest gift we can give to the world is our love, given freely and unconditionally.

Any person's knowledge or perception is not this. Human beings tend to be conditional. If our children are nice, we love them. If they misbehave, we withdraw our love from them and sometimes get angry with them. God would never do that. To be like God, we would need to continuously love our children, irrespective of how they behave. There would be no exceptions. Our children would be taught discipline through love, not through fear of punishment. Humans are above all very conditional about life. We love life, when it brings good things to us. We hate life, when it brings disagreeable things to us.

O Dear One, in this way, one becomes Shiva. In this way, means one has to be unconditional like God. To practice this verse means that our nature has to be like God's – unconditional, not dependent on external causes or circumstances. Yoga gives the beautiful example of a lotus flower to explain this concept. The lotus flower lives in water. It is found in water. Yet, if you touch a lotus flower, you will find that it is dry. Even though the lotus flower lives in water, it is unaffected by it. We are to apply the same principle to our lives. Even though we live in this world, we are not to be affected by it.

When we apply this to our lives, we decide to be happy, or joyful, or love, irrespective of our external circumstances.

Whatever the circumstances of our life, we always choose to be happy or joyful. To practice this, awareness is required. When we are not aware, we will give the same conditioned response to every situation in life. When we are aware, we can choose our response to every situation in life. There is a very similar message also given in the *Conversations with God* series of books by Neale Donald Walsch. *Conversations with God* says that what we are being is totally within our control. It does not have to be a reaction to the external world. Our state of being depends on our decision to be something. We can decide to be happy, or peaceful, or loving, and we will be that, no matter what happens in our lives. To practice this, you should direct your attention back towards yourself, to what you are being. Whatever you are being (sad, depressed, etc.), change it. Be happy, or joyful, or loving. Maintain your awareness on what you are being throughout the day. Even when you are talking to someone, remain aware of what you are being. If you find yourself thinking, or getting upset, or sad, stop and change what you are being. Again become happy, or joyful or loving. This is the way to practice this verse. In this way, one will remain happy or joyful throughout the day, in response to each and every circumstance in life. In this way, we are being like God throughout the day. When you are like God, you become God – you realize your true nature.

100

Consciousness is the essential quality in all bodies. There is no difference anywhere. Therefore, everything is made of the same consciousness. By understanding this, a person is victorious over worldly existence.

Mystics have always maintained that all matter, all bodies are composed of energy. Energy comes from consciousness, therefore all bodies are essentially consciousness. When you understand this, you stop identifying with the gross form of your body. Instead you identify with consciousness. Then, you immediately become aware. You become peaceful. You are able to live your life, without being affected by any external event. Whatever is happening is happening to your body. All your worries used to concern the body. Now these will end. Now, you identify with awareness. You are merely the witness, observing all the events of your life. It does not matter any longer which way your life works out, because ultimately none of this affects you. You are consciousness, not your gross body or your ego.

To practice this, believe you are awareness. You will then be aware. Continue to be aware, continue to be a witness. You will start identifying more and more with awareness, and less with your ego or body. Ultimately your ego will disappear, and you will be free. This process does not take long. The Ashtavakra Gita says that it can happen in an instant. All it takes is for you to believe that you are consciousness. That the gross form of your body that you see is not real. Your body is actually nothing but consciousness. When you believe you are consciousness, your belief will turn into reality. When it does, you will be free.

Consciousness is God. Therefore, this verse can also be read in the following way – *God is the essential quality in all bodies. There is no difference anywhere. Therefore, everything is made of the same God. By understanding this, a person is victorious over worldly existence.* When you understand this, your whole life will change. When everything is made of the same consciousness, or the same God, how can one thing be superior to another? Everything is Divine. We normally consider ourselves superior because of our money, achievements, race, country, religion, gender, caste, etc. This verse points out that none of these divisions are real. We are not Hindu, Muslim, or Christian. We are not Indians or Americans, or Chinese, or any other nationality. We do not belong to any caste or gender. We are all consciousness or God.

Everything in this universe is made from consciousness. That means that human beings are not superior to birds, or to animals, or to any other objects. All objects, animate or inanimate, are composed of consciousness. Nothing is superior or inferior because they are made of consciousness – they are all made from the same thing. We normally treat a rich or famous person with greater respect than a poor or an unknown person. In truth, no one is superior to anyone else. They are all made from the same consciousness.

The feeling of superiority leads us away from God. When we feel superior, we strengthen our ego, and that only makes it more difficult to realize our Self. People who feel superior often behave in the most inferior ways towards those they consider inferior. There are countless examples of this. It can be seen in the behaviour of religious extremists. They treat minorities in a terrible manner. In truth, superiority is a fiction. It is an illusion. Everyone and everything is made of the same God.

101

When strong emotions of desire, anger, greed, infatuation, intoxication or jealousy appear – stop the mind! By doing that, the True Reality underlying those emotions, appears.

Emotions are nothing but energy (energy in motion). Energy is neutral. It can take on any form. Desire, anger, greed, etc. are all forms of energy. This verse emphasizes strong emotions. When strong emotions appear, it means that energy has been raised to a very high level. You will notice this immediately with people who are angry. They seem energized, capable of lashing out.

stop the mind! When these strong emotions appear, suddenly stop the mind. You are having thoughts of anger, violence, or greed, or jealousy. Suddenly, quit them. Simply be aware. *Remain aware.* This energy that has arisen, has no option but to go back to its Source, to God. When it returns to God, it takes you with it.

The difficulty in practicing this verse is in being aware that a strong emotion has arisen. It is only when you are aware that a strong emotion has arisen that you can stop the mind. The problem is that usually a person who is angry or greedy, is one who has lost awareness. If you are in a state of awareness, you will never be angry or greedy or jealous, in the first place. If you are being these things, it means that you have lost awareness. Then one has to regain awareness when these emotions are in full swing, so that one can stop the mind. Usually this does not happen. One is so engrossed in these emotions, that one loses all awareness. However, sometimes one can become aware that one is being angry or greedy, etc. Then, this meditation can be practiced.

꧁ 102 ꧂

See the whole world and all its separate moving objects, as a magic show, or an illusion, or like a picture. From this meditation, joy arises.

We think that the world is real, and that is why we suffer. Our mind continuously thinks and worries about our lives, and events taking place in this world. But if you realized that the world is nothing but an illusion, you would stop thinking about it. The mind would then fall silent and you would be liberated.

See the whole world and all its separate moving objects, as a magic show, or an illusion, or like a picture. The world is an illusion. Because we believe it is real, it appears real. Now the verse asks us to change our belief and our perception of the world. Believe the world is unreal. Then the door will be opened to experience Ultimate Reality. See the world as an illusion, or something unreal. You would stop thinking so much about it. Instead you will be a witness, watching the passing scenes of life. When you watch a movie, in the end you know that it was just a movie. Nobody got hurt, nobody died, nothing bad happened. It is the same with this world. Nothing real ever dies. People do not die, they only change form. The body may pass away, but the eternal self lives on. When you know the world is an illusion, and nothing of value is destroyed, you live your life in a new way. You lose all your fears, and live freely. You are no longer affected by the events taking place in your life or in the world.

Changing our perception can be a very powerful way of stilling the mind. That is all that this verse is doing. If you think the world is real, you will be overly concerned about it, and you may keep thinking about the events occurring in this world and in your life. Now if you perceive or believe that the world is unreal, you will immediately stop thinking about it. Why would you think about something that is unreal? The mind on its own would fall silent. No effort would be required. Instead of thinking, you will now simply be aware, living fully in the present moment.

From this meditation, joy arises. All our worries, all our problems concern our body or this world. When we know this world is nothing, what problems or worries can we have? Our lives become joyful. This sentence also refers to the time when the mind falls silent. When that happens, the joy of our true nature automatically appears.

Enlightened masters have frequently said that we live in a dream world. What appears so real to us is actually unreal. Some masters have also said that the world is a creation of our mind. The world, as we see it, does not really exist. Statements like this have always puzzled people. How can the world be an illusion when it appears to be so real? The objects around us seem so solid and real. Once again, the example of a movie is useful in understanding all this. When we see a movie, the images on the screen are created by the film passing through a projector. If we switched off the projector, then we would no longer see the various images, we would only see the screen. The mind is like that projector. When you "switch" off the mind, or are able to control it, then you no longer see the diversity of life. Instead, you see the unity of all existence. When the mind is stilled, we experience Ultimate Reality. We see life and the world as it actually is, not as it previously appeared to us. The world as an objective reality ceases to exist.

☙ 103 ❧

One should not place their thoughts on pleasure or pain. O Goddess, know that True Reality lies between the two.

The Katha Upanishad says that the soul is attracted to two paths – the path of pleasure and the path of joy. Those who follow the path of pleasure, go from life to life, and do not reach the Supreme. Those who follow the path of joy reach the other shore, and are liberated. This verse is teaching the same thing – do not be attached to pleasure or pain. There is no salvation there.

There are other texts that also state that attachment to pleasure does not lead to salvation. The Ashtavakra Gita says that life after life we indulge in different pleasures, only to lose them all. It then advises that we should stop all this. Lord Krishna in the Bhagavad Gita says, "Contact with the physical world brings pleasure and pain, heat and cold. But Arjuna, they are transient; they come and they go. Have patience, O son of Bharata." (2:14) When we live life through our sense organs, we experience pleasure and pain. To reach God, we have to transcend the world of pleasure and pain. How do we do this? We do this by detaching from all the information we receive from our sense organs. Instead, we turn within and look for joy within ourselves. This is a message this text gives repeatedly. When we are no longer affected by the external world, then the external world ceases to have any power over us. Then, we become a master.

Pleasure and pain are transient, they are not real, and they do not last. That is why this verse tells us not to place our thoughts on them. Do not waste your time on something temporary. It does not lead to everlasting happiness. For lifetimes we keep seeking pleasure. This pleasure is always short lived. It is usually followed by pain. You cannot have pleasure without pain. If you have a mountain, you must have a valley. So, for many lifetimes, one continues with this cycle. We seek pleasure that is obtained for a short period, only to be followed by pain. This pleasure-pain duality continues for our entire life, or for many lifetimes, till we finally seek something higher.

O Goddess, know that True Reality lies between the two. What lies between pleasure and pain? The state of awareness and joy. That is where we find True Reality. When we are aware, we experience pain and we experience pleasure, but we do not suffer. Suffering comes from judgement. We judge pleasure and say it is good, and we judge pain and we say that it is bad. A master never does that. He or She is simply aware. He experiences pleasure and pain without judgement, and therefore does not suffer. When we live life through our body or ego, we are constantly reacting to the external environment. Pleasure feels good and we like it. Pain feels bad, and we dislike it. The master has no ego, and therefore there is no like or dislike. She is constant. She is always joyful.

When one reads a sentence that says that one should be unaffected by pleasure or pain, one may think that this means one should be like a machine with no feelings or emotions. This is incorrect. It means one should by joyful irrespective of one's external environment. Life is to be celebrated, totally and completely. Even when life does not look good. One is not to live like dead men. One is to celebrate and enjoy life every minute of the day. That is what this verse is telling us. One is not to enjoy life when there is pleasure, and dislike life when there is pain. One is to enjoy life whether there is pleasure, pain or anything else. That is why the second path the Katha Upanishad talks about is the path of joy. This is the path that leads to God. It is the path of being joyful regardless of what is happening in the external world. In this path, the world ceases to have any power over you.

Osho also explained this beautifully. He said that we always have a choice whether to be unhappy or happy, miserable or joyful. We may not have control over external events, but we always have control over how we react to them. Why choose to be unhappy when you can be happy? Why choose to be miserable when you can be joyful? The wise are the ones who choose to be joyful.

Lord Krishna was one who demonstrated this truth in his life. He was always joyful, always celebrating life. This is a side of his life that is not highlighted today. Instead, only his message given in the Bhagavad Gita is given importance. Yet, his life lived, was a demonstration of the truth he taught in the Bhagavad Gita. It is okay to celebrate life, it is okay to enjoy life, it is also okay to enjoy the pleasures of life. Do not think that this verse says that one should not enjoy the pleasures of life. Tantra would never say that. What this verse means is that one should not be dependent on them for one's happiness. Enjoy everything, but need nothing external for your happiness. Everything you need to be happy or joyful, you will find within yourself. The pleasure you obtain from the external world cannot compare with the joy you will find within. The Brihad-aranyaka Upanishad discusses this at length. It says that if you take all the pleasures of the world – fame, fortune, power, etc., you can consider that to be one unit. Now as you progress spiritually, the joy you experience within keeps growing. The Brihad-aranyaka Upanishad quantifies this joy at each stage, and it is several times more than the pleasure you experience from the outside world. Finally, the joy of liberation is quantified at a million times a million (1000 billion) more than the sum of all the pleasures you can experience in the external world!

How does one practice this verse? First, one should not think about pleasure or pain. Instead be aware, live life in the present. Once you reach a certain level of awareness, you will automatically be joyful. Alternatively, as Osho and the Katha

Upanishad say, one can *be* joyful. Be aware of what you are being, and change that so that you are joyful. Remain aware of what you are being throughout the day, so that you remain joyful. A time will come, when you are fully aware, and totally joyful. In this way, you take the path of joy to God.

☙ 104 ❧

Leave behind concern for one's body. With a firm mind and vision for nothing else, believe – "I am everywhere." Then, one will attain joy.

We believe we are the body, and that is why we feel bound. It is our belief that we are our body that prevents us from seeing our True Nature. This is one of many verses in the book that tries to break our attachment to the body. It gives us a new belief to believe in and practice. Believe that we are everywhere. This is the truth about our nature. We are a part of God, and God is everywhere. Therefore, we are also everywhere. This verse gives us a new thought, a new idea to believe in. The new belief is an accurate description of our Real Nature. It unlocks the door to eternity. When practiced, this belief slowly turns into reality. When it does, we are liberated.

Leave behind concern for one's body. By all means take care of your body and try to prevent illnesses. But see the body as a tool. Do not regard it as your Real Self. This is what the verse is saying.

With a firm mind and vision for nothing else, believe – "I am everywhere." Incorporating a new belief is different from practicing a sitting meditation. A sitting meditation is practiced for a certain period of time each day. A new belief is an idea you hold throughout the day. It is not that you think of this belief, "I am everywhere", once a day, and then start thinking about something else. No, it is a belief you must continuously hold throughout the day. Then, the belief will turn very fast into reality. The verse says only think about this belief, and do not think about, or have a vision of anything else. An example from the ancient Indian epic, the Mahabharata, will make this clear.

King Drupada arranged a ceremony, to find a suitable husband for his daughter Draupadi. Many great warriors and princes were invited. Whoever would be able to pierce the eye of a fish with an arrow, by watching its reflection in water, would win Draupadi's hand in marriage. One was not allowed to watch the fish directly, but only its reflection in water. The fish was circulating above, and the water was placed below on the floor. A person had to look down, and shoot the arrow upwards. Many great warriors tried and failed. Arjuna was the only one who succeeded. When he was asked how he succeeded, he answered, "I could only see the fish's eye, and nothing else."

This is the single-pointed focus one should have while practicing this verse. Believe that you are everywhere. Do not think about or believe anything else. In a very short time, this belief will turn into reality, and you will be free.

There are many beliefs given in this text that can liberate us. They can all be practiced with the single-pointed focus given in this verse. Then, results will be obtained very fast. This single-minded focus can also be used to attain other goals in life. You may have certain other aspirations in life. Then think only of that goal, and nothing else. You will obtain your objective very fast.

ଔ 105 ରு

"Knowledge, desire, etc. exist not only within me, but everywhere in jars, and other objects." With this belief, one becomes omnipresent.

This verse is a variation of the previous one. *"Knowledge, desire, etc. exist not only within me, but everywhere in jars, and other objects."* In Kashmir Shaivism, God is said to have three main energies. The energy of knowledge, the energy of action, and the energy of will or desire. The words, knowledge, desire, etc. used in this verse refer to the energies of God. What the verse is basically saying is that God's energy exists not only within me, but everywhere, in jars and other objects. There are two things implied in this sentence. First, I am not my body, I am energy – the energy of God. Second, this same energy exists everywhere, in jars and other objects. Therefore, all matter, living or inanimate, is composed of energy, God's energy. Nothing else exists, only God's energy exists. This energy is everywhere. Everything is composed of this energy. Since I am nothing but this energy, and this energy exists everywhere, I am everywhere.

This verse is basically saying the same thing the previous verse said – believe I am everywhere. The difference here is that this verse is giving the truth behind this belief. It is explaining the reason why this belief is true. Everything in the world is nothing but God's energy. Since you are this energy, you exist everywhere. The verse can also be read in the following way – *Energy exists not only within me, but everywhere in jars and other objects.* Or simply put – *I exist everywhere,* or *I am everywhere.*

With this belief, one becomes omnipresent. When you believe you are omnipresent (exist everywhere), you become omnipresent. A belief has to become reality. There is no other choice in this matter. Whatever we believe must become real. When we believe we are omnipresent, we become omnipresent. We realize our true nature and become God.

☙ 106 ❧

The awareness of object and subject is common to all living beings. However, the yogis have the distinction that they are always aware of the self.

This is a beautiful verse, and a very important one. It defines what awareness really is.

The awareness of object and subject is common to all living beings. Everyone is aware of the subject-object relationship between themselves, and other objects. We consider ourselves to be the subject, and everything else that comes into our sensory field as objects. If we are talking to someone, they are the object, and we are the subject. Similarly, if we are looking at some mountains, or the sea, the mountains and the sea are the objects, and we are the subject.

However, the yogis have the distinction that they are always aware of the self. To be aware, some of our attention has to be directed back towards ourselves. If 100% of our attention is directed outwards, we are lost in objectivity. This happens to most people, throughout the day. For example, if you are talking to someone, usually you are totally engrossed in the conversation. You are not aware of yourself speaking. Your attention is 100% towards the object, the person you are speaking to. You are then 100% lost in objectivity.

To be aware, to be in a state of awareness, some of your attention has to be reversed. It has to be redirected back towards yourself. Douglas Harding called this "reversing the arrow of attention." Normally our attention is only pointed outwards. Now, some of this attention is pointed back towards ourselves. When this happens, you become self-aware. When you are talking, you are aware of yourself talking. When you are eating food, you are aware that you are eating food. When you are listening to someone, you are aware of yourself listening. To be aware means to be a witness. You are constantly aware of what you are doing, and how you are reacting. Our true self is this witness, (our soul) not our body or ego. When we are aware, we are in our true state. When we are lost in thoughts or in objectivity, then we are not in a state of awareness. The longer we remain aware, the more our awareness grows. When we reach full awareness, we reach our highest state.

How much attention should be redirected back towards ourselves? It varies from time to time. There is no fixed rule. Sometimes, you will find almost 100% of your attention is directed towards yourself. At other times, most of your attention is directed outwards and very little towards yourself. What is important is that at least some of your attention is directed towards yourself, even 1%. Unless that happens, you are not in a state of awareness, you are lost in objectivity. To be aware means to be aware of the self. That is what this verse is saying. Sometimes, being aware is also defined as being a witness. They both mean the same thing. When you are aware of the self, you are a witness, and you are in a state of awareness.

However, the yogis have the distinction that they are always aware of the self. The way to practice this verse is given in this sentence. Always remain aware of the self. Simply put, always remain aware. The emphasis is on always. One has to remain aware, one has to maintain the state of awareness. If you get lost in thoughts or in objectivity, become aware again. To be aware or aware of the self, means to live in the present. Thoughts take us to the past or the future, and then we are no longer aware of the self. The term yogi in the verse is meant in a broader sense. It does not just mean someone who practices yoga. It also means someone who is enlightened. The difference between an enlightened person and others is that the enlightened person is always aware. Therefore, be a yogi. Become aware of the self. Remain aware throughout the day. Whether you are eating, drinking, bathing, talking, walking, watching a movie, or doing anything else, remain aware of the self. Some of the earlier verses taught us to be aware of our breath, or what we are being, throughout the day. Those verses were also teaching us to be aware of the self. To practice this verse, one can also be aware of one's breath, or what one is being (joyful, love); or simply just be aware of the self.

When you remain aware throughout the day, you will find a definite change in yourself. When you are aware, it becomes impossible to continue certain types of behavior. Anger, greed, violence, fear, hatred, etc., will disappear from your life. You can only be angry or fearful, when you lose awareness. It is impossible to be angry or be anything negative, when you are aware of the self. An angry person is one who is totally lost in the situation, or in objectivity. He has lost awareness of the self.

There are some beautiful verses in this text that define yoga. That show us the main teachings of yoga. This is one of them. *However, the yogis have the distinction that they are always aware of the self.*

☙ 107 ❧

Leaving aside concern for one's own body, one should continuously believe that the same consciousness is present in oneself and also in other bodies. In a few days, one will be all pervading.

Yoga and tantra say that all matter is nothing but energy. And energy comes from consciousness. Therefore, all matter is consciousness. If you look deeply at matter, you will find energy. If you look deeply at energy, you will find consciousness. There are some verses in this text that say our body is nothing but energy. There are others that say that we are in essence nothing but consciousness. They mean the same thing. It depends how you look at something.

Leaving aside concern for one's own body, one should continuously believe that the same consciousness is present in oneself and also in other bodies. To practice this meditation, the first thing to do is to detach ourselves from our gross body. Set our body aside, and stop believing we are the body. Instead, we are to believe we are consciousness. The same consciousness that is present in us is also present in other bodies. We are part of an infinite body of consciousness that exists everywhere. Everything is made from this consciousness. You may find it easier to understand this verse, if instead of consciousness, you use the word God. *One should continuously believe that the same God is present in oneself and also in other bodies.* This is the basic theory of non-dualism. That only God exists. Everything is made of God, everything is a part of God. God is in everyone and everything.

One of the modern messengers of God, Neale Donald Walsch, in his *With God* series of books, explains non-dualism in a simple and beautiful phrase – *We are all One.* That is all that this verse is saying. We are all One. The same consciousness or God is present in us and in other bodies. We are not separate from each other and we are not separate from God. Only God (or consciousness) exists. We are all part of the Whole. We are all a part of God. We are all One. This is a message that God has been sending us for centuries. The Isha Upanishad says, "He who sees all beings in his Self and his Self in all beings, thereafter has no fear." The Ashtavakra Gita says, "Realizing the Self is in all beings and all beings are in the Self, brings about the birth of the enlightened sage." Finally the Bhagavad Gita says, "He who sees Me everywhere and sees everything in Me, then I never leave him and he never leaves Me."

To practice this meditation, continuously believe that we are all One. The emphasis in the verse is on continuously. A belief must be continuously maintained throughout the day. When you do this, it becomes strongly ingrained in you. The stronger the belief becomes, the faster it turns into reality. This is a belief that has to be practiced. Treat others as if they were part of you. Treat others as if we are all one. Your behavior towards everyone else will change dramatically. You would not hurt or abuse yourself, or be angry with yourself. Now you will stop doing these things to others. You will no longer see others as "others", but as a part of you. You will then stop treating other people with violence, fear, hatred, jealousy, or any other negative emotion. Instead, you will treat them with kindness, love, compassion, forgiveness and understanding. You would do this because this is how you would treat yourself. And now you would see everyone as a part of yourself, and you as a part of them.

Sometimes people are unkind to us, or create problems or difficulties in our life. Our normal reaction is to dislike that person, or get angry with that person. The next time this happens in your life, say to yourself, "I am that person." (*the same consciousness is present in oneself and also in other bodies*). Immediately, all your anger and hatred will disappear. You will treat that person with respect and love, and often receive a similar reaction from them. The Ashtavakra Gita explains this beautifully:

You are in whatever you see.
Just you alone.
Do bracelets, armlets and anklets of gold,
appear different from gold?

The world only arises from your ignorance.
In reality, you alone exist.

There is no one,
no living being and not even God,
separate from yourself.

There is a very significant difference between religion and tantra, or religion and the philosophy of non-dualism. Religion seeks to change you through a system of reward and punishment. If you are good, you go to heaven. If not, you go to hell. This gives rise to expectation. And expectation in our daily lives can cause frustration and suffering. If we are nice to people, we expect them to be nice to us. If they are not nice to us, then we get upset. We think, after all we have done, this is how we are treated. Tantra, on the other hand, is very different from religion. It does not seek to change your behavior through a system of reward and punishment. Tantra seeks to change you completely. To change you from the core of your being. To make you a nice, or kind human being. When you are a kind person, you automatically do what kind people do. Kind people do kind things not for any reward, but because that is who they are. If someone is not kind to you, you do not care. You continue to be kind, because that is a reflection of who you are.

When you understand and practice this belief of unity – we are all one, you will understand the deeper meaning of the wonderful statement of Jesus Christ – Do unto others as you would have others do unto you. You would do to others, what you would like others to do for you, for the simple reason that you and the other are one. What you do to others, you actually do for yourself. What you do to others, you will one day experience. If you cheat someone, someone in the future will cheat you. On the other hand, if you give love, you will receive love. This in a nutshell, is also the Law of Karma. This law works for a simple reason – there is no other, there is only One. Whatever you think you are doing to others, you are actually doing to yourself. Whatever you give or send out, comes back to you, because there is no one else. If you want to receive love, then give love, be love. An abundance of love will then be received by you.

People sometimes are unhappy with their jobs or their relationships. The relationship could be with their parents, spouse, children, or anyone else. The important point to understand is that we only get back what we give. We cannot expect to receive any happiness from our jobs or our relationships, if we do not put any in. Take the example of a mirror. A mirror reflects our image. It shows us how we are. If we have put on weight, it will show that, and if we have lost weight, it will show that too. The world is something like that. It simply reflects to us, or gives back to us, what we put in. To experience more happiness in our jobs or our relationships, we have to give more happiness. The true source of happiness is internal. It is when we are being happy, and giving happiness, that we receive it. The external world merely reflects our inner state, and returns to us what we give.

This is also the reason why masters say, you don't end hatred with hatred, you end it with love. Whatever energy you give out comes back to you. If you are receiving hatred, you should give back love. Then you will receive love. This is a principle that is applied to all of life. A fire cannot be doused with fire, it is put out with water. And violence is not ended with violence, it is ended with non-violence.

☙ 108 ❧

O Deer Eyed One, by stopping all thoughts, the mind will be without support. Then the self will become the Supreme Self of God.

The body needs food, water and air to survive. Without these three things, the body would not survive. What does the mind need to survive? The mind needs thoughts to survive. Thoughts are to the mind what food, water and oxygen are to the body. The mind feeds on thoughts. Every time you think, you strengthen the mind. The mind is nothing but a bundle of thoughts. On the other hand, when you remain aware, you weaken the mind.

O Deer Eyed One, by stopping all thoughts, the mind will be without support. Stop all thoughts. Whenever you become aware that you are thinking, stop thinking, and come back to the present moment. This is something you may have to do several times a day. Practice this even when you are facing a problem. It is our thoughts that create bondage and suffering in our lives. Even if you are having pleasant thoughts, thoughts you enjoy, stop those thoughts and return to awareness. The happiness you feel from thinking pleasant thoughts is very limited compared to the peace and joy you feel when the mind is stilled.

When you try and stop your thoughts, you start thinking less. The interval between thoughts starts increasing. With fewer thoughts, your mind becomes weaker. A time comes when the mind suddenly collapses and disappears altogether. It is like weakening the structure of a building. You remove parts of the structure bit by bit. That is what you are doing here by having fewer thoughts. Eventually the structure becomes so weak, that the whole building collapses. That is what happens with the mind when you practice this verse. This entire process does not have to be as gradual as described above. Some people are able to stop thoughts, and control their mind very quickly. It depends on how determined or intent you are. It only takes a few minutes of having no thoughts for the mind to be stilled forever.

There are many diseases known to mankind – diabetes, cancer, malaria, asthma, etc. The seriousness of the disease has varied through the ages, depending on whether mankind has found a cure for it. One of the worst diseases is the disease of uncontrolled thinking. Even the medical profession now admits that our thoughts can affect our health. Thoughts of anxiety, hatred, fear, violence, greed, impact our health in a negative way. On the other hand, thoughts of love, mercy, joy, happiness, affect our health in a positive way. Uncontrolled thinking can be considered a disease, for a deeper reason. Our thoughts prevent us from experiencing the incredible and infinite joy of our true nature. All our misery and suffering is due to thinking and its related offshoots, such as judgement, expectation, or condemnation. When we are simply aware, there is no judgement, there is only experience. Consequently, there is no suffering. More important, when the mind is stilled, we experience the joy of our true nature. Our real nature is pure joy, infinite joy. The mind acts like the wall of a dam. It checks us from experiencing and expressing the joy of our nature. When you break the wall of a dam, the surrounding areas are engulfed with water. Something similar happens when the mind is stilled. You become engulfed with joy, and everyone around you can feel this joy.

When you stop the mind and live in awareness, you live life in the present, from moment to moment. You accept everything that comes into your life, no matter how negative it may seem. You develop a deep sense of trust in God. You understand that things work out perfectly for you. Whatever comes into your life is only there to help you evolve, and move you closer to your true nature. You even accept your own death with equanimity, knowing that this is what is best for you. Lord Krishna put this beautifully in the Bhagavad Gita, when he said, "That which first seems to be poison, is found in the end to be the highest nectar. That happiness is pure. It is said to be born from a clear perception of the Self." (18:37)

Then the self will become the Supreme Self of God. If you stand in front of a mirror, you can see yourself. However, if the mirror has a layer of dirt covering it, you would not be able to see yourself. You would have to first remove the layer of dirt. The mind is like that layer of dirt. It is only after it is removed that you can see your Real Self. When our mind is stilled our ego disappears, and God appears. Our limited self vanishes, and our true Divine nature unfolds. We become God in flesh.

༄ 109 ༅

God is omniscient, omnipotent and omnipresent. Believe firmly, "I have those same qualities of God." Then, one becomes God.

We are all a part of God, and God is a part of each of us. God is our true nature. Our ego is our illusory nature. Our ego is limited in terms of knowledge, power and presence. On the other hand, God is all knowing, all powerful and all pervading. In this verse, we break our identification with our ego by changing our belief. We are to believe we have the same qualities of God. That we are omniscient, omnipotent and omnipresent.

The verse says *believe firmly*. This means to believe continuously, and without wavering. All beliefs turn into reality. How quickly they do so, depends on how deeply ingrained they are. This belief should be maintained throughout the day, with full faith and conviction. Do not allow negative thoughts to settle, and do not let your mind seduce you into thinking that this is impossible. That you cannot be omniscient, omnipotent and omnipresent. It is impossible for your ego to be these things, but it is not impossible for the Real You. The Real You is God. And God has all these qualities.

The best way to firmly incorporate this belief is to practice it. Start with knowledge or omniscience. If you are perplexed or puzzled by something in life, seek the answer by going within. Ask yourself the question, and then give yourself the answer. You may ask yourself the question at night, and then give yourself the answer in the morning. You may also do so after a shorter duration. You can even give yourself the answer immediately. When you give yourself the answer, you will be surprised at the wisdom you have within. It is then that you will realize that the inner source is omniscient, and that you are in fact omniscient. Use this verse. It has many practical benefits. Ask yourself important questions about life. What job to take, who to marry, how to solve a particular problem. And then use the wisdom within you, to lead you through your life.

You can even apply this verse by using omnipotence. Do not try to move a mountain or attempt to lift a car. Even though some masters have shown that they can perform miracles, you may need to grow substantially in your evolution, before you can make the same claim. Instead, start with something small. Something that may first seem outside your reach. There are several examples of people who overcame severe obstacles to reach a goal in life. They had the strength and the power to carry on, where others gave up. Give yourself a task or goal to achieve which you initially feel may be beyond you. It could something simple like learning a new language, or learning how to change a car tyre. Then set yourself out to achieve your goal and don't take no for an answer. Do not think of failure, and do not accept failure. You will surprise yourself with your inner strength and abilities, and with how easily you sometimes achieve your goal. You will then come to a wonderful new conclusion about yourself – that there is nothing that is beyond your reach if you set your heart and mind to it.

The more you experience the truth about this belief, the

quicker it turns into reality. One becomes more and more omniscient, omnipotent and omnipresent.

Then, one becomes God. When one believes one is God, one becomes God. That is what this verse is doing here. By believing we have the qualities of God, we are in effect believing that we are God. The more we believe we are God, the less we believe we are our ego. As this belief turns into reality, our ego disappears, and we become God.

❧ 110 ❧

Just as waves arise from water, flames from fire, light from the sun – in the same way, the various forms of the universe have arisen from Me, God.

This is a beautiful verse. It teaches us so much, using such a simple example. A wave arises from water. It has no separate existence. It is nothing but water. If the wave only saw its form, it might get scared. It would think it has a beginning and an end, a birth and a death. Once the wave realizes it is only water, it will no longer be scared. Water has no birth or death. It is the same with every form of the universe. Each form of the universe has no separate existence. It has arisen from God. It is nothing but God, just as a wave is nothing but water. When you understand this, fear goes away from your life. You cannot be destroyed. You are a part of God, and have no birth or death. Your body may be destroyed, but you will not be. You will only change form. You are a part of God, and you will live forever.

When you realize your life is eternal, you will live your life in a new way. You will find it easier to detach from the world, and from any problems you might face. How significant can any problem be, when you know that you live forever? You will also not cling onto experiences that you enjoy. You will realize that life goes on forever, and any experience that you miss will be possible to re-experience again in the future. When you understand this, you are able to detach from the world. It then becomes easier to still the mind. That is when you realize your true nature.

There is another very important lesson this verse teaches us. A wave arises from water and is full of water. It is nothing but water. A flame arises from fire and is full of fire. It is nothing but fire. In the same way, we (and every form of the universe) arise from God, and are full of God. We are nothing but God. God is love and joy unbounded. God is an infinite amount of love and joy. Since we are full of God, and nothing but God, we are also limitless love and joy. Now, if you were to ask a wave to look for water, would a wave look outside itself? That would be ridiculous. A wave is full of water, it is nothing but water. It would only need to look within itself to find an abundant amount of water. The same is true of human beings. Human beings are nothing but love and joy infinite. Yet, isn't it ridiculous that we look for joy outside ourselves, and not within? We only need to look within to find an abundant amount of joy, love or happiness. The joy we find outside, is nothing compared to the joy we find within. The Brihad-aranyaka Upanishad goes to the extent of saying that the joy we find within is 1000 billion times more than any joy one can experience from the outside world.

The outside world is important, make no mistake about that. Without the outside world, we would not be able to experience the joy within. If we only experienced the joy within, after a while our experience would be void, nothing. We need a relative field, a contextual field, to provide a contrast. The world does that. You cannot continuously have one experience, without having the opposite experience. You cannot know what total joy is unless you experience something less than total joy. In the absence of something less than joyful, you cannot experience total joy. The world is there so that you can have all kinds of experiences. It provides a contrast so that you can experience the joy within. But the idea is to find the ecstasy and joy of our true nature within. We will not find that in the external world.

There are three things to learn and practice from this verse. First, believe we are God, and everything else is God. We are nothing but God. We are not our ego or our body. Just as the essence of the wave is water, and not the form of the wave, in the same way our essence is God, and not our gross form. This belief will turn into reality. When you no longer identify with your ego or your body, your ego starts dissolving. Once your ego is gone, you will realize your true nature. Second, once you understand that you are a part of God, you will realize that you live forever. This will help you detach from the world, and move towards God. Third, look for joy within and not outside. There are enough techniques given in this book, to show you how. When you look for joy within yourself, you take a giant leap forward in your evolution. The external world no longer affects you, because you are no longer looking at the external world as a source of happiness. Instead you find the source within you. You are the source of joy, love or happiness.

There is one other very important lesson to learn for this verse – that only God exists. There is no reality other than God. Every form of the universe arises from God, is filled with God. This is the heart of the philosophy of non-dualism. This is a point that is touched upon directly, in some of the later verses.

☙ 111 ❧

One should swiftly turn his body round and round, till he falls to the ground. At the end of the energy of motion, the Supreme State is born.

When you swiftly turn your body round and round, you become dizzy. You continue to do this, until you cannot do it any more, and fall to the ground. When you are lying on the ground, exhausted and dizzy, you cannot think. Your mind is automatically silent. This is an important moment. The door to eternity has just been unlocked. To open it, you have to be aware. This is a golden moment. The mind is silent. It is now possible to see your Divine Nature. To do so, you must remain aware. Awareness is what leads you to your highest state. If you are not aware, then this moment will pass. And then, within a short while your mind will be thinking again.

☙ 112 ❧

When there is lack of energy or lack of knowledge, the mind is dissolved, and one is absorbed into energy. In the end, when the energy subsides, God appears.

There are some moments in life, when the mind automatically becomes still. These moments are rare, and must be seized. They can quickly take one to their highest state. In order to seize these moments, one has to be aware. When the mind is still and one is aware, one is quickly liberated.

The first instance occurs when there is lack of energy. When one is very tired or exhausted, the mind falls silent. This is because to think requires energy. Sometimes, one is so tired that one does not even have the energy to think. In these moments, a person just wants to lie down and recover their strength. These are rare moments. The mind has fallen silent on its own. To take advantage of these moments, one has to be aware when these moments arise. Then, one is swiftly led to God. Otherwise, if there is no awareness, these moments pass. Then the body recovers its strength and the mind starts thinking once again.

The mind also falls silent, when there is lack of knowledge. This situation arises when one is stunned, or shocked, or in a state of disbelief. This can happen when your life is in danger. Someone pulls out a gun on you. People who have experienced life-threatening situations always remark how time seems to slow down in these moments. Time almost stands still. Admittedly, when your life is in danger, the last thing you will be concerned about is your spiritual liberation. Yet these moments have great possibilities. If you are aware during them, you will be swiftly liberated.

There can be lack of knowledge not only when your life is in danger. These moments can also arise, when you are witnessing an event happening. You may witness a car accident, or some event that stuns you into disbelief. It does not have to be a negative event. It can also be something joyful. You are watching a sports event, and something incredible happens. A particular athlete may perform in a particular way that changes the whole course of the sporting event. There can also be lack of knowledge when someone asks you something. You are dumbfounded by what you have been asked. You cannot believe that someone can ask you something like that. You are stunned into silence.

There are several examples like these that one can give. These moments do not occur everyday. They are rare. If one has their wits about them, and can be aware, then one can use these moments to reach God.

the mind is dissolved, and one is absorbed into energy. In the end, when the energy subsides, God appears. This refers to the ascent of Kundalini. When the mind falls silent, and one is aware, then the mind permanently dissolves. Kundalini rises up through the center of the spine. When it reaches the top of the head, one is liberated. Then, God appears.

☙ 113 ❧

O Goddess, listen carefully, as I explain the mystic tradition. If one's eyes are fixed without blinking, unification with the Supreme, will occur immediately.

The practice of keeping the eyes fixed without blinking, is called Bhairavi Mudra. It was a secret technique of tantra, possibly because it was very powerful, and produced results in a short period of time.

To practice Bhairavi Mudra, one has to fix their eyes without blinking and direct their attention inwards, towards one's self. In other words, one has to be aware of the self, while the eyes are fixed without blinking. The movement of the eyes is somehow connected to the thought processes. This is something the ancient mystics of India discovered. If you do not move your eyes, you stop thinking. To think, there has to be movement of the eyes. If you stop the movement of the eyes, you stop thinking. This process can happen very fast.

When you first practice this, your eyes may tire quickly. You may feel the need to close them. When this happens, you can blink, or close your eyes briefly. Then reopen the eyes, and continue with the practice.

ଓ 114 ଓ

Close the ears, and compress the opening of the rectum. Then by meditating on the sound without vowel or consonant, one permanently enters God.

The sound without vowel or consonant is the sound of silence. Silence is the opposite of sound. It is the absence of any sound. Silence is our true nature. It is in silence that we find God. In silence, the mind is still. In silence, the ego is absent. By meditating on silence, we are meditating on our true nature. It is therefore a direct way to reach our true nature.

The practice of compressing the opening of the rectum is called Ashwini Mudra. It is used to prevent the escape of energy, and to redirect it upwards for spiritual purposes. When you practice this mudra, you should take care to avoid tensing any other part of the body. Sometimes when people practice Ashwini Mudra, they inadvertently tense their waist or their legs. This should be avoided. If you find it difficult to practice Ashwini Mudra, you should omit it from this practice. You can also practice this meditation without doing Ashwini Mudra. Then, in effect you will be practicing Verse 38.

To practice this meditation, sit comfortably and close your eyes. Then close the ears. This is done by pressing the small outer flap of the ear against the opening of the ear, with any of your fingers. Maintain this position for the rest of the practice. Then close the opening of the rectum, by performing Ashwini Mudra. Maintain Ashwini Mudra for the rest of the practice. Now, focus on the silence within. By closing the ears, all external noise is blocked out. One now has to concentrate on the silence within. Sometimes stray thoughts may disturb the silence. When thoughts arise, ignore them. Focus once again on the silence.

By concentrating on silence, the mind becomes silent. This is a natural phenomena. We are attracted to silence because it is our true nature. It is also in silence, that we feel very peaceful. It is a feeling we start longing for. What a relief it is to have the mind silent. There are no thoughts, just silence and peace. After a while, you eagerly look forward to your meditation. All external noise is blocked out, and all internal noise is stopped by focusing on the silence. Then, there ensues a beautiful feeling of peace. Peace that turns into joy, and joy that eventually turns into bliss. Bliss of union with God.

Peace comes automatically with silence. It has to. It is a part of silence. It is noise that disturbs us. There are also certain sounds that soothe us, and there are some sounds that take us to God. One of the best amongst these is the sound of silence.

115

Stand over a deep well, etc. and look without blinking at the deep hollow space. The mind becomes completely free of thoughts, and then the mind is immediately dissolved.

This meditation is similar to some of the meditations given earlier in the text. It works in three ways. First, by looking without blinking, all thoughts stop. By stopping the movement of the eyes, we stop the flow of thoughts. Second, by looking at a deep well, we are only seeing darkness. There are no other objects that one can see. The mind needs an object to think about. When there are no objects to think about, the mind automatically falls silent.

A third important factor here is that, our ego needs another object by which to differentiate itself by. We get our sense of self, or sense of separation, by looking at other objects, and seeing ourselves as different from them. But what if there is no other object to look at? Then the ego has no support, and it collapses. Just as the mind needs thoughts to survive, the ego needs other forms, other objects to survive. When no other forms or objects exist, then the ego ceases to exist. One's true nature then appears.

Stand over a deep well, etc. and look without blinking at the deep hollow space. Etc. refers to any other deep, dark hole. It can be a well or some other hole. What is important is that it should be deep and dark, so that no other object is visible. There is only darkness. When you practice this, you will have to position your face at the edge of the well, so that you only look into the well. You should not be able to see anything else, even from the corner of your eye.

☙ 116 ❧

Wherever the mind goes, externally or internally, everywhere there is the form of Shiva. As God is omnipresent, where will the mind go?

The philosophy of non-dualism holds that there is only God. Only God exists. Everything you come in touch with through your senses is full of God, is a part of God. When you understand this truth deeply, your life changes. That is what this verse is about. It changes your perspective.

When you understand there is only God, most of your desires fade away. Earlier you categorized people, events, or material things as more special from one another. Certain people were more special for you, certain events and memories were cherished more, and certain material objects were given more value. Your immediate family or your close friends were more special than people you did not know. Certain objects, such as jewelry or expensive cars, were given more value than objects of less monetary value.

Now if you come to understand that everything is only God, then everything and everyone is given equal value. Everyone is special. No one is less or more special than anyone else. Every object and every form is only God's energy in different shapes and sizes. It's all the same energy. God's energy cannot be more special than itself. When you understand this, you stop preferring one thing over another. After all, it's all the same thing. You cannot prefer the same thing to itself.

Wherever the mind goes, externally or internally, everywhere there is the form of Shiva. Everything the mind thinks about – every internal or external form, person or object, is only a form of God.

As God is omnipresent, where will the mind go? When you know there is only God, what is there to think about? The mind on its own falls silent. For us to think about different people or objects, we have to see them as distinct, separate entities. That is why we think so much. We see objects and people as separate from each other, with their own individual identities. Now, when we realize that what we are seeing is an illusion, and everything is only a form of God, our perception changes. We no longer see form, we see substance. We no longer see separate entities, we see One Whole. To think, the mind needs different objects to think about. When you only see One, how can the mind think? Even if there was two, you could think. You could compare one with the other. Now that is not possible. There is nothing to think about – where can the mind go?, as the verse asks.

To practice this meditation, you have to understand and believe that there is only God. You have to behave that we are all part of this One. When you genuinely believe there is only One, there is only God, your whole perception changes, and your mind automatically falls silent.

☙ 117 ❧

Whenever awareness is increased through any sense organ, remain in that awareness. Then, the mind will be dissolved and one will be filled with the Supreme Self.

There are moments in our life when our awareness is increased, in response to our external environment. This can happen through any sense organ. We can hear a piece of music we love, and suddenly our attention picks up. We see something beautiful, and our awareness increases. It could be beautiful scenery, a beautiful person, or an object that we are attracted to. What happens next is that our awareness increases. We stop thinking and become aware. The verse asks us to maintain that increased level of awareness. We can experience higher levels of awareness in response to our external environment. Once experienced, it can be maintained. We sometimes lose awareness. However, it is possible to regain awareness and move to higher and still higher levels of awareness. That is the beautiful thing about awareness – it can never be permanently lost. It is our true nature. One can be aware again by simply deciding to be aware.

Then, the mind will be dissolved and one will be filled with the Supreme Self. People often make the mistake of thinking that salvation is difficult and requires a few lifetimes' worth of effort. This belief, like all other beliefs, becomes self-fulfilling. Actually, at any given point of time, we are only a moment away from salvation. This text repeatedly makes the point that without thoughts, the mind loses its support, and dissolves.

It only requires the mind to be without thoughts for a brief period of time for it to disappear forever. It depends on the intensity of one's desire to be free. The greater the desire, the faster one is liberated.

☙ 118 ❧

At the commencement and end of a sneeze, during danger, sorrow, weeping, flight from a battlefield, during curiosity, at the commencement and end of hunger. These states are full of the State of God.

What is so special about these states? At the commencement or at the end of a sneeze. During danger or sorrow. At the beginning or end of hunger. How are these states full of the state of God? These states are special, because during these moments the mind on its own becomes silent. In any of the moments described in this verse, the mind is quiet. Sometimes it is because of a shock – during danger, sorrow, or retreat from a battlefield. At other moments, it is due to a natural phenomena of the body. Just as we begin to sneeze, or just as a sneeze ends. You will notice that during these moments the mind does not think. Something similar also happens with hunger. When you start to feel hungry, at that moment there are no thoughts. It is the initial moment, when the feeling of hunger first arises. Similarly when hunger ends. You were feeling hungry and now you take that first bite of food. At that moment, you feel some joy, some fulfillment, as you start to end your hunger.

During all these moments, the mind becomes silent. To make use of these moments, one should *be aware* when they occur. These are the two critical words missing in the verse. One should be aware when these moments arise. It is during these moments that the path to God can be seen. The mind has fallen silent and the door to eternity has been opened. However, if you are not aware when these moments arise, then this golden opportunity will be missed. These moments pass, and the mind starts working again. Then, one returns to a normal state.

When the mind falls silent, we can get insight into our Divine Nature. To receive this insight and realize our true self, awareness is necessary. Awareness is always the key to our salvation. When we are aware, the mind is silent. But when the mind has fallen silent on its own, due to an external shock, and we are aware at that time, then there is a greater chance of us permanently remaining aware.

119

Leaving concern for one's body, remember the sight of a place, object or incident. The mind will be without support and one experiences a flood of Divinity.

The important thing to understand about this verse is that it makes us into a witness. It uses memory to make us a witness. When we are a witness we are not thinking, we are simply observing. When we are a witness, we no longer identify with the body or the ego – we identify with the soul. It is our soul that is a witness. In the state of awareness, a person is always a witness. We are usually aware of the present moment. In this verse, we are using our memory to become aware of a past place or incident. The principle is the same – one is aware, one is a witness. The difference here is that one is aware of the past.

Practice this meditation sitting comfortably, and with eyes closed. Now remember a past place or incident. Choose something enjoyable. Use a memory that you are fond of. You may choose to remember something of your childhood. You may practice this in two ways. You may remember a past experience through your own eyes. In this way, you will relive or re-experience that incident from your original point of view. Or you may see it as an outsider. In this case, you will be like a third party, also observing yourself and all others involved in that incident. Choose whichever method you find easier to practice. This is applicable only if you are remembering a past incident. If you are remembering a place, then you will remember it the way you originally saw it. Then the first method will be used.

When you practice this, try and remember every small detail of what happened. If it is an incident from your childhood, relive every moment of it. If there were excited people around, try and capture the feeling of excitement present in the air. Relive the whole moment in its fullest detail. If it's a place that you are remembering, particularly one that you are fond of, see it once again in detail. If there were mountains there, capture the majesty of the mountains, the freshness of the air.

Remembering our past can be exhilarating, especially if it is of fond memories. When we come back to the present, we come back with a sense of happiness. Sometimes people keep remembering their past to escape something they do not like about their present lives. It could be a handicap they are suffering from, or a financial condition they are in. When you practice this meditation, your awareness will increase. This increased awareness will be used daily in your present life. With increased awareness there will be increased joy and happiness. You will then awaken to a wonderful new truth – all the joy you require is available inside you. Then, even though your external situation remains the same, you would have changed. You will live your life with a new sense of joy and happiness and freedom. The external world will no longer have any power over you. You will also understand the true meaning of salvation or freedom. To be free means to be independent – independent of the external world for our happiness.

120

After looking at some object, one should slowly withdraw their sight from it, then their knowledge together with their thought of it. O Goddess, one will then reside in the Void.

This practice enters a void through an object. First, one has to look at an object. Then, one slowly withdraws their sight from it. This is done by slowly closing one's eyes. Next, one has to slowly stop all thoughts or feelings about the object.

When this is done, there is *shunya* or void. There is nothing. One is silent, still.

Some people find it difficult to straightaway become still. This practice leads them into stillness in a slow, gentle way. One goes step by step into the void. Choose an object you are fond of, or something that attracts your attention. First, look at the object for a brief period of time. Then, slowly withdraw your sight from it, by slowly closing your eyes. After closing your eyes, there still may be some thoughts or feelings on the object. Gently stop all thoughts or feelings for the object. Then, there is only silence, stillness. Continue to be aware of the silence or stillness. You may repeat this process a few times till you are deeply into the silence.

We have to empty our mind of all thinking, all cluttered thoughts. When you look at an object, you are focusing only on one object. You are thinking only of one object, not of several objects. This is an immediate improvement. Instead of thinking of several things, we are now only concerned about one object. The next step is to stop thinking of anything, to stop thinking altogether. So, the process is to go from thinking of several things, to thinking of one thing, to thinking of nothing. For some people this may be easier than going directly from thinking about several things, to thinking about nothing. This meditation focusses all our thoughts and attention first on one object, and then on nothing.

☙ 121 ❧

From an abundance of devotion and a detached nature, an understanding of Shiva's Energy is born. One should continuously be her. Then, Shiva.

The path of devotion is a very noble path. It is found in most religions. Devotion in this verse simply means love. It can also be devotion to a particular deity. Devotion to a particular deity is a beautiful path, where one dissolves rapidly.

The verse also stresses detachment. One has to have an abundance of love and a detached nature. What this means is that one has to love unconditionally. One's love should not be given only in certain situations to certain people. Instead, it should be given freely, all the time, independent of the events of one's life, or the external world. This is possible only with a detached nature. If you do not have a detached nature, then your love will be conditional, not unconditional. Then you will love life only when it brings things you enjoy. You will not love life when it brings things you do not like. True love is always unconditional. Conditional love is a poor substitute. Love is infinite and free.

What does it mean to be unconditionally loving? A few examples are given in spiritualism to explain this. To be unconditionally loving means to be like the sun. The sun shines equally on everyone, irrespective of their race, color, gender, religion, caste, nationality or personality. In the same way, one should love people of all types. No moral judgements should be passed. One should love all equally – people who society calls good and people who society calls evil. Krishna explains in the Bhagavad Gita, (5:18) that one should have the same evenness of love for an upper caste brahmin, a dog, and a man who eats a dog.

The breath is also used to explain the concept of unconditional love. We breathe spontaneously throughout the day and night, irrespective of the circumstances we find ourselves in. Whether we are being loved, attacked, rebuked or praised, we continue to breathe. We breathe during every possible situation or event that occurs in our lives. We need to love in the same way – during each and every moment in our lives. It does not matter what is happening to us, or to our world. We must love at every moment, just as we breathe in every moment. That is the meaning of unconditional love. It does not depend on any condition. Even when we are attacked, we give love. Even when we are made to look foolish, we give love. Love is our response to every situation in life.

an understanding of Shiva's Energy is born. Shiva's Energy is the Goddess. What is the understanding? The understanding is that the Goddess is love. Some verses in this text say that God (and the Goddess) is joy, and others, like this one, say God is love. Love and joy can be used interchangeably. They mean the same thing.

One should continuously be her. One should continuously be love. At every moment of the day. It is important to understand that what we are being does not necessarily have to be in response to an external event. Usually we react to the external world. If some events that we dislike occur, we become upset or angry. If events that we enjoy take place, we become happy. However, it is important to realize that what we are being is within our control. It does not have to be in response to the external world. It actually depends on our decision. If we decide to be love or peaceful, we will be. Even if events occur that we term as undesirable. It is our inner reaction that is important. External events are not always in our control. But our inner response to them is always in our control. That is what a master is. A master is one who has mastered himself (or herself). They have control over their emotions. They decide what they want to be in response to every situation in life, and they remain that, no matter what.

There may be certain situations in your life that you do not enjoy. It could be something simple as taking out the garbage, or preparing your tax returns, or meeting a particular individual. The next time you face these situations in life, decide to experience them in another way. Choose to love them, or choose to be love while experiencing them. Then, you will discover one of the greatest secrets of life – you can experience life in any way you choose.

One of the greatest masters who showed this was Jesus Christ. There are three things people fear the most – death, pain and loss of wealth. Christ experienced two of these at the same time. He was tortured to death on the cross. He was experiencing pain, and he was dying. Yet even in that moment he had nothing but love. He made that famous statement on the cross – "Lord, forgive them, for they know not what they do." Jesus Christ was a fully enlightened saint. He performed many miracles, and could have stopped what was happening to him at any time. But through the last moments of his life, he sent a very powerful message to the world – that even in your darkest hour you can love. This is a message he gave through the example of his life and his death. "Come, follow me", he said. There is no better way to follow him than to be like him. To be love, through every moment of one's life.

Jesus Christ is believed to have lived in Kashmir for some years. The meadow he lived in, Yusmarg, is named after him. It is impossible to say whether Christ was influenced by Kashmir Shaivism but some of his teachings are similar to those of Kashmir Shaivism.

ଓ 122 ଓ

Understand an object is empty inside. Emptiness is also a feature of all objects. With mind free of thoughts, meditate on that emptiness. Then, even though the object is perceived or known, one becomes calm.

Emptiness or void, is a very important concept in the philosophy of non-dualism. Emptiness means that an object is empty of a separate self. *Understand an object is empty inside.* An object is empty of a separate existence, of a separate self. Yet, it is full of God. This is the key concept to understand. An object looks separate. It seems that it has a separate existence. But this is an illusion. It does not have a separate existence. It has no separate self. It is only God in a different form. From a thread, one can make various types of cloth. Yet all those forms of cloth are nothing but thread. In the same way, all objects are nothing but God. *Emptiness is also a feature of all objects.* All objects are empty of a separate existence, but are full of God.

With mind free of thoughts, meditate on that emptiness. Choose an object. Close your eyes and meditate that that object is an empty shell. It has nothing inside. It is one with all of existence. Continue to meditate in this way.

Then, even though the object is perceived or known, one becomes calm. Later, after you complete the meditation, you will still see the object. But now you have come to a new understanding. You now realize that the object is not separate from you or from God. It is a part of God, just as you are a part of God.

123

That considered to be pure by people of little understanding, is neither pure nor impure in the Shaiva system of philosophy. One who rises above dualizing thoughts attains complete happiness.

The next few verses are beautiful. They get to the heart of the philosophy of non-dualism.

That considered to be pure by people of little understanding, is neither pure nor impure in the Shaiva system of philosophy. The Shaiva system of philosophy refers to the non-dualistic philosophy of Kashmir Shaivism. Yoga, tantra or Kashmir Shaivism, are very different from other religions. Parts of Hinduism was for a certain time blighted by the caste system. The upper caste brahmins considered themselves to be purer than members of the lower castes. During certain parts of the menstrual cycle, women were considered impure, and were not supposed to visit temples.

Kashmir Shaivism used to scoff at all these practices. Kashmir Shaivism says that what you consider pure is God, and what you consider impure is also God. Therefore, how can something be pure or impure? In non-dualism, there is only God. Every object in this universe is God. God cannot be pure or impure. God is God. A brahmin is a part of God and a member of the lowest caste is also a part of God. So how can a brahmin be pure and a member of the lowest caste be impure? A man is God and a woman is also full of God. Therefore, how can men be purer or superior to women? They cannot. The Kashmir master, Abhinavagupta, used to give the example of Ganga water and wine. In Hinduism, water from the river Ganga is said to be pure and sacred, and wine being alcohol was said to be impure. Abhinavagupta said that there was no difference between Ganga water and wine. God was in both of them. One was not purer than the other.

There are several examples of pure and impure found in our world today. Members of one religion consider themselves to be pure (and superior), and consider members of all other religions to be impure. The concept of pure and impure can be highly dangerous, as the world is finding out today. From purity and impurity comes superiority and inferiority. People who consider themselves pure, also consider themselves superior to those they call impure. Those who consider themselves to be superior immediately start treating those they consider inferior in an inhuman way. The Nazis thought their Aryan race was pure and superior. They then tried to destroy or dominate members of other races. The same thing happens with religious fundamentalists. They consider their religion superior, and then try and destroy or convert members of other religions.

One who rises above dualizing thoughts attains complete happiness. This is the key to practicing this meditation. Rise above thoughts of separation, thoughts of dualism. Do not see the world in terms of good and evil, pure and impure, you and God. Instead see everything as One. See all of life, all of existence as a part of God. Almost all suffering, all misery, comes from a feeling of separation. The more you feel one with God, and with all of life, the more joy you will experience in your life. Therefore, do not see yourself as separate. Instead, see and experience the world and everything in it, as part of One Whole. It is because you see yourself as separate that you remain separate. When you believe you are one with God, you become one with God.

124

"God is existing everywhere, common in all. There is nothing else other than God." With this knowledge, one attains the non-dual condition.

This verse sums up the philosophy of non-dualism. That only God exists, and nothing else exists. This is all that we really need to know – there is only God, and we are all one with God and each other. When you know this and understand this, you change. And then your life changes. If you think you are separate, you may have anxious thoughts about your survival, and your day-to-day needs. When you know that you are one with the Whole, you realize that the Whole (God) will take care of you. You also know that your survival is guaranteed. You are part of something eternal and infinite that cannot be destroyed.

When you realize that you are One with God, your ego starts dissolving. You also stop fighting with life. You surrender to life, you accept whatever comes into your life, knowing that it is for your own good. This surrender or acceptance of life is important. It is your ego that fights with life. Life can be compared to a river. A river flows to the ocean. It has to. It has no other choice. In the same way, life leads us to God, to our true state. When we fight with life, we try and swim upstream. We struggle so hard, and then we realize that we have made no progress. When we surrender and accept life, we find ourselves being led rapidly to God. When we accept life, our life suddenly starts working. Instead of us struggling to achieve goals, life starts bringing us things of its own accord.

The concept of surrender is often misunderstood. People sometimes feel that to surrender is to resign oneself to one's fate in life. This is incorrect. To surrender means to accept whatever life brings us without labeling or judging it in any way. One can then seek to bring about change without being attached to the final result. For example, a family member may fall sick and may require urgent medical help. To surrender in this situation does not mean that we do nothing. Surrender means, that one calmly accepts the situation without getting upset or worried, and then acts and takes decisions to help one's family member. You will find that when you are calm and peaceful, and your emotions are under control, you are better able to take decisions in the best interests of all parties concerned. It is when we refuse to accept life, and we allow the external environment to disturb us, that we sometimes act in ways that we later regret.

Surrender also has a deeper meaning. It means to surrender to God's will, and to allow the process of life to work through us. We are never separate from the Whole, we are never separate from God. Therefore, it is always in our highest interest to follow the Whole than to fight with the Whole, to follow God's will, than our own separate will. When we surrender, we become an instrument in the hands of God, and we perform actions that are ordained of us. Ramana Maharshi used to say that we are like actors on a stage, who perform the roles that are given to us. With surrender we immediately become peaceful, and we no longer identify ourselves as the "doer". We lose all our fears, and we understand that with God's help there is nothing we cannot achieve, and no obstacle that we cannot overcome. When we let God into our lives, we realize that it is not necessary to worry and extensively plan our lives. Instead, we can surrender to God, and allow God to lead us through our lives. When we surrender, we develop a deep sense of trust in the process of life. Instead of thinking about the future, we live in the present moment, focusing on our response to each moment of life as it occurs.

When you realize that all of life is one, you stop hurting yourself by hurting others. This is the advice that Krishna gave in the Bhagavad Gita. When there is only One, what you are doing to someone else, you are actually doing to yourself. What you cause someone else to experience, you will one day experience. If you give love, you will receive love. If you are violent, you will receive violence. This is also called the Law of Karma by some. It is a law that you cannot avoid. You may escape the laws of your country, but you can not escape the Law of Karma.

To practice this meditation, believe that you are one with God and all of life. Behave with others as if they were one with you, not as someone separate. If you thought someone else was one with you, wouldn't you treat them differently? You would start treating everyone with love and compassion and kindness. And then you will find that the more love you give out, the more you will receive.

It is our thoughts of separation that create misery and unhappiness in our lives. Our ego makes us feel separate. When you give up the ego, you stop being affected by life, and start accepting it fully. You become a witness, watching life take its course. Therefore, believe you are one with God. Like all beliefs, this will also turn into reality. As it does so, pain and suffering will disappear from your life, to be replaced with ever increasing joy.

☙ 125 ❧

From knowing that God completely fills everything, one is the same towards enemy and friend, in honor and dishonor. With this attitude, one obtains joy.

Kashmir master, Abhinavagupta, used to teach his pupils that if you hate anybody you hate God, because God is in everybody. He would then quote this verse from the *Vigyan Bhairava.* This is a very high level of understanding, and a beautiful way of explaining Ultimate Reality.

If you met God tomorrow in the street, in human form, wouldn't you be really happy? Would you not treat God with love and respect? Well, open your eyes and look around you. Everyone and everything you see is God. Now try and treat them that way.

We normally have difficulty treating everyone as God, because sometimes people behave in ungodly ways. This is because they have forgotten who they really are. We see a Hitler, or a Stalin, or a Pol Pot, all of whom butchered millions of innocent people, and we wonder how these people can be divine. Yet people like them and many others, have forgotten their true identity. The fastest way to make them remember is to treat them for who they really are. Not to judge them for their past misdeeds, or to judge by appearances. But to recognize their real nature and to treat them with love. When you recognize someone for their real nature, and treat them accordingly, there is a greater chance that they will recognize themselves and their true identity.

The beauty about tantra is that it changes your behavior by first changing you. This is the only way that the change in your behavior becomes permanent. Religions, on the other hand, try and change your behavior with a carrot and stick policy. If you are good, you go to heaven. Otherwise, you go to hell. Fear is not the best way to induce permanent change in a person. Tantra changes your perception. When you perceive everyone as divine, you treat them that way. When you perceive that you are divine, you behave in a Godly way. When you perceive everyone is a part of you (we are all one with God and each other), you treat others the way you treat yourself. Religions teach us that we are born in sin. No good can come from such a teaching. If we feel bad about ourselves or guilty about ourselves, we lessen the chance of doing something good to ourselves or to others. On the other hand, when we know that God fills us completely, and that we are divine, we start behaving in a divine manner.

We practice this verse by changing our perception. We normally perceive individuals as separate entities. Therefore, we respond to them depending on how they treat us. We love a friend and hate an enemy. If we now perceive everyone is God (God fills everything completely), we will treat everyone the way we treat God. We will treat everyone with love and respect, and we will treat them this way *irrespective of how they treat us.* Love is our real nature. The more we love, the faster we return to our highest state.

Everything is a part of God. When we realize that God fills us completely, we understand that we have Everything within us. All the love and happiness we desire, we have within us.

It does not matter what part of Everything shows up in our external life. Whether it is honor or dishonor, pleasure or pain, we remain unaffected by it all, knowing that all we need, we have within us. We then accept life fully, and remain peaceful and joyful through all the moments of our life. When we accept life fully, our ego dissolves and we realize our true nature.

☙ 126 ❧

There should be no feeling of aversion or attraction towards any person or place. By remaining in the center between the two, one is liberated from the duality of aversion and attraction. Then, one experiences God spreading everywhere.

When you feel aversion or attraction for any person or place, it means that you are living life through your ego. It is the ego or our body that likes or dislikes. Our true self or our soul, does not like or dislike. Our true self is awareness and joy. Awareness and joy is what is in the center between aversion and attraction.

To be liberated, one has to set the ego aside. The way to do this is to be a witness, and to accept whatever life brings us. It is our ego that sometimes resists life. It likes some things and dislikes others. When you accept life fully, you no longer live life through your ego – you live life through your soul, or your Real Self.

This does not mean that one should not have desires or goals in life. One can have desires and work towards them, but one should not be attached to them. Our happiness should not depend on our desires being fulfilled, or on us being able to change our external life situation in a particular way. One should accept whatever life brings us. This is one of the most important messages that Krishna gave in the Bhagavad Gita. He said, don't be attached to results. The Maitri Upanishad also says that if we are attached to things of this world, we are bound. If we are free of them, we are liberated. Neale Donald Walsch explained all this in a modern context, in his book, *Friendship With God. Friendship With God* says that one should elevate our addictions to preferences. We should not be addicted to a particular result, we should prefer a particular result. Next, we should elevate our preferences to acceptance. We should accept whatever appears in our lives.

Events in life take place, so that we can rapidly realize our true nature. Whatever events are taking place in our lives are only taking place to help us realize our highest nature. There is no other reason for them to take place. It is the same with people. Whoever enters our life, good or evil, does so only to help us evolve. There is no other reason for them to enter our life. When we understand this, we immediately let go and stop resisting life. We drop all our fears, and instead flow with life, enjoying every moment of it, knowing that it is all for our highest good. When we do this, every event becomes a blessing, every person becomes a saint, and every moment becomes joyful.

God is in every person, place or thing. Therefore, the nature of every person, place or thing is the same. When we understand this, why would we prefer one person or place to another? Why would we like one person and dislike another? To do so would mean that we have got lost in the world of duality or illusion. Instead, one should not judge by appearances. One should be of even mind to all people and places. One should love all people, all places and all events equally. That is how one rises above the world of dualities – by being singular in our behavior, and our response to all situations in life.

The ancient sages of India used to explain all this with the example of a lotus flower. The lotus flower grows in mud and water. Mud is ugly, and the lotus is beautiful. From something so ugly, comes out something so beautiful. It just goes to show that the same energy (God's energy), is in what we call ugly and what we call beautiful. When we understand this, we stop judging things (persons, places, etc.) by their appearances. Instead, we see them for their essence. Appearances may differ but the essence of everything remains the same. When you understand this truth, you respond in the same way towards different people and different places. Then, as the verse says, you become liberated from the duality of aversion and attraction, and you experience God spreading everywhere.

☙ 127 ❧

That which is beyond knowledge, beyond grasping, beyond not being, that which is void – contemplate all that to be God. In the end, the birth of enlightenment.

There are certain characteristics given to God in this verse. God is *beyond knowledge.* Our knowledge is limited and based on cause and effect. God is not based on cause and effect. God is supportless and requires no cause or condition to exist.

Beyond grasping. God is not an object that can be grasped or held. God is like air – free flowing and all pervasive.

Beyond not being. God is eternal. God never ceases to exist, never ceases to be.

That which is void. Void here means that God is infinite, and not limited to a particular person, or at a particular place. When we use the word "God", we tend to limit God. We immediately think of some superior person, living in heaven, watching every move of ours. Instead, think of God in terms of a quality, such as love or awareness. Love or awareness is infinite, and is not limited to a particular person.

Practice this as a sitting meditation. Close your eyes, and meditate on God to be all these things – supportless, all pervasive, eternal and infinite. Meditate on God not as a particular person, but as something that has all these qualities. As we do so, we start acquiring those very qualities. As the Bible says, we are made in the image and likeness of God. Because we think of God as limited, as a particular person, we think of ourselves as limited, as a particular person. When we drop these false notions of God, we drop the same false notions about ourselves. Then, we realize our true nature.

☙ 128 ❧

Fix the mind on external space, which is eternal, supportless, void, all pervasive and silent. By doing this, one will completely enter non-space.

Space has several qualities similar to God. Space, like God is eternal, supportless (requires no support or condition to exist), void, all pervasive and silent. In the previous verse, one had to meditate on God who is supportless, all pervasive, eternal, and infinite. In this verse, we meditate on space, which has the same qualities.

Practice this as a sitting meditation. Focus your attention on external space. Feel yourself becoming one with this space. Feel that you are also eternal, supportless, void, all pervasive and silent.

This meditation helps to break our identification with our body. Our body is a tool or vehicle we use to experience life, and our true nature. We are not our body. This is a point this text makes repeatedly. Our true nature is eternal, infinite and supportless. By practicing this meditation, we stop identifying with our body, and instead start remembering our true nature – we become eternal, infinite and supportless.

When you deeply understand that you are not your body, you lose all fear. Then you realize that all life is eternal. You never die, you only change form. Sometimes we feel fear, when our family, our nation, or our religion is threatened from outside. This fear goes away when we realize that we are eternal. Take the example of a pot or jar. A pot or jar may break, but the air inside it never gets destroyed. Similarly, our body may get destroyed, but our True Self within the body, never gets destroyed.

ଓ 129 ଡ

Wherever the mind goes, at that very moment, one should leave that thought. By not allowing the mind to settle into thoughts, one will be free of thoughts.

Whenever you find yourself thinking, immediately stop thinking and come back to the present moment. That is what this verse is teaching us. The mind always takes us into time. Our thoughts are always about the past or the future. The present moment is not a part of time – it is a gateway to eternity. In the present, the mind cannot exist. We are simply aware. The present moment is a present, a gift from God. It is in the present that we reach God. Yet we keep ignoring this present. We let our mind take us to the past or the future. However, God is always there for us, waiting for us in the present moment. If only we could make ourselves available in the present, we would be able to meet God. Yet, usually we are not present, we are absent. We are lost in the past or the future.

This is an important meditation practice that will have to be used sometime by everyone. It does not matter which meditation you are doing. You will occasionally find yourself thinking. You will then have to practice what this verse is teaching – you will have to stop thinking and come back to the present moment, and to your meditation practice.

By not allowing the mind to settle into thoughts, one will be free of thoughts. The mind has a habit of thinking continuously. By stopping thoughts whenever one notices they have arisen, one breaks this habit. Then the mind falls silent. This is the greatest gift you can give yourself – the gift of silence. Silence of the mind. One then experiences the incredible joy of one's true nature.

Most people make the mistake of believing that money is the solution to all their problems. The more money one has, the happier one will be. That is why books on how to make money or become rich, are very popular. Actually, our happiness is not dependent on anything external. The more control you have over your mind, the happier you will be. The fewer thoughts one has, the more aware one becomes. With greater awareness, one experiences greater joy.

People are sometimes scared of living in the present. They feel that they have to constantly think about their future, and plan for all the various problems they might face. Actually, all this thought is unnecessary. Most stress and anxiety are due to our thoughts about the future. We are facing an immediate problem, and start visualizing various bleak scenarios that may result from this problem. Or we worry about other problems we may face in the future. What people do not understand is that all this thinking and worrying makes one feel miserable in the first place. Therefore, why think about all these things?

Instead, deal with life one moment at a time, and deal with each situation as and when it arises.

We sometimes fail to realize that there is a far greater intelligence than our mind, running the universe, and our lives (if we allow it to). We must try to align ourselves with God's will, and flow with life rather than resist it. When we live intensely in the present moment, we know in each moment of now what action needs to be taken, or whether any action needs to be taken. Life becomes helpful, and solutions and coincidences appear that allow us to solve our problems, and move forward in our lives.

The ancient Greek philosopher Epictetus taught that external events on their own do not disturb us. It is our thoughts about them that cause us unhappiness. Once we stop our thoughts, we are at peace. He also said that we suffer when we want things to be different from what they are. Therefore, the key to our happiness lies not in controlling the external circumstances of our lives to our complete satisfaction (which is impossible), but in controlling our minds, so that external conditions do not bother us.

The first thing we do when we face a problem is actually the last thing we should do – that is to think and worry. We worry because we think we are separate from God. When we understand that we are one with God, we realize that God will take care of us. Aurobindo put it beautifully when he said, "Worrying is not having faith in the Divine." A master lives life from moment to moment, and is happy with whatever shows up in her life. She realizes that all events are a blessing and a gift that leads one to God. Sometimes circumstances we call undesirable are a blessing that may not be apparent until much later.

☙ 130 ❧

God gives rise to everything, pervades everything and every sound. Therefore, by continuously reciting the word Bhairava, one becomes Shiva.

God is everything. Everything and everyone comes from God, and God is in everything. By chanting the name of God, we are lead back to the Source of all creation.

One can practice this meditation by chanting Bhairava verbally, or in one's mind. Bhairava is one of the names of Lord Shiva.

Chanting a mantra or a name of God has many benefits. The most important one is that it stops the mind from thinking. The name of God has a certain power, a certain energy. It directly leads one to their true nature.

☙ 131 ❧

"I am, this is mine, etc." On the occasion of this assertion, let the mind go to that which is without support. From the impelling force of this meditation, one attains Peace.

Either our ego can exist, or God can exist. There is no room for both. There is room only for one. To realize our divine nature, we have to get rid of our ego. When we empty ourselves of our ego, we realize that we are filled with God. But first we have to remove our outer covering, our ego. Then, we see the treasure hidden within.

"I am, this is mine, etc." On the occasion of this assertion, let the mind go to that which is without support. You will notice two realities within you. One is your mind that keeps on chattering or thinking inside. This is your ego. It is unreal. The second is the witness. You can observe yourself thinking. You can also observe external events. Who is this observer? This observer is your soul. It is the part of God that is within you. This witness is God. This is your Real Self. You can try a little experiment now. Normally, you are lost in thought. This is our ego-self thinking. Now observe yourself thinking. See what thoughts arise. Be a witness to these thoughts. Now you have two selves. One is the thinking self (ego), and the other is the witness (God).

This verse says that every time your ego asserts itself, let your mind go to that which is without support – let your mind go to the witness in you. Your ego asserts itself by saying, "I am this", or "I am that", or "this is mine". Whenever this happens, be aware or be a witness. Then, you will stop identifying with your ego. You will start identifying with the witness in you. Slowly, slowly, your awareness will grow and your ego will become weaker. One day, your ego will disappear altogether. That is when your Divine Nature will unfold.

☙ 132 ❧

"Eternal, omnipresent, supportless, all pervasive and Lord of the Entire Universe." By meditating every moment on these words, in conformity with one's object, one obtains one's object.

To understand this meditation, one has to first understand the second part of this verse. What does the verse mean when it says that one should meditate every moment on these words in conformity with one's object? What is one's object? One's object is to be liberated, to realize one's true nature. That is what this entire text is about. If one's object is to be liberated, then how should one meditate on these words, so that this object is achieved? In what way should one meditate on these words, so that one is liberated? The way to do this is to say "I am" before the first part of this verse. That is, one should believe, "I am eternal, omnipresent, supportless, all pervasive and Lord of the Entire Universe."

Meditate *every moment* on these words – "I am eternal, omnipresent, supportless, all pervasive and Lord of the Entire Universe." The emphasis is on every moment. One has to believe this every moment of the day. It is then that this belief quickly turns into reality. We believe we are the body, and that is why we feel separate. We are actually not our bodies. We are a part of God. We are God. We are eternal, omnipresent, all pervasive as the verse says. This is our true nature. All these qualities, eternal, omnipresent, etc., are qualities of God. And we are not separate from God. That is why we are all these things too. Whatever God is, we are too.

Our senses create our beliefs, and our beliefs create our reality. This is a point that needs to be understood. It helps explain this verse and the next, and several other meditations given in this text. Our sense organs give us inaccurate information. They do not show us the full picture. Based on the inaccurate information received from our senses, we form inaccurate beliefs. Our beliefs create our reality. This is a point discussed earlier in this book. Our inaccurate beliefs show us an inaccurate reality. For example, if we relied only on our senses, we would believe that the sun rotated around the earth, and also that the earth was flat. In fact, both these beliefs were held as truth for many centuries, until we received more information. Then, we changed our belief. We realized that the earth was round, and that it rotated around the sun. Similarly, because of our senses we see our body and think we are the body. We also see the boundary of our bodies and believe that we are separate entities, separate from the rest of life, and separate from God. Both these beliefs are inaccurate. Both these beliefs create our reality, a false reality. We believe we are separate, and therefore, we remain separate.

The way to undo all this is to ignore the information received by the senses. Instead, adopt a new belief that runs counter to our sensory perceptions, but gives a true picture of Ultimate Reality. That is what this verse and many of the verses in this text do. They give us new beliefs to adopt that open the door to eternity. These new beliefs turn into reality, and liberate us. It is important to remember this – to reach God, we have to go beyond the information our sense organs give us.

☙ 133 ❧

The entire universe is not real. It's appearance is an illusion. "What is real about an illusion?" From believing this firmly, one abides in Peace.

☙ 134 ❧

The Self is unchangeable. Where is there knowledge or activity? External existence or objects are dependent of knowledge. Therefore this world is void.

Verses 133 and 134 are not two separate meditations. They are one meditation. The universe is not real, it is an illusion. What we are seeing, the way the world appears, is an illusion. This is a point that has been made earlier in the text, and it is an important point to understand.

Do not believe everything the senses show you. This is the first point to understand. Because we believe in the information the senses give us, we are attached to this world. We get affected by all the events of our lives. We react positively or negatively to events, depending on how we judge them.

This verse asks us to change our belief. Do not believe that the world is real. Instead believe it is unreal, it is an illusion. When we believe this firmly, we immediately become peaceful, as the verse says. When we believe the world is not real, we become detached from it. External events no longer affect us. The mind falls silent. The mind keeps thinking because it gets affected or agitated by external events. When we believe the external world is an illusion, the mind falls silent. When the world is not real, what is there to think about? Why think about things that are not real? The mind on its own falls silent. We then, become a witness. We watch the events of life as we watch a movie – totally unaffected by the outcome. When the mind falls silent, we reach our highest state.

When you realize the world is an illusion, you are no longer addicted to your desires. You may still have desires, but you are no longer attached to results. You do not care whether a particular desire materializes or not. You are now happy because you have now decided to be so. You are no longer happy or unhappy as a response to situations in life. You have now become a master – a master over yourself and a master over life.

To practice this verse, anytime you feel you are being affected by an external event, say to yourself – "This world is not real. It is an illusion." You will immediately feel peaceful. Practicing this meditation requires courage. If you told a mother who had just lost her child, "Don't worry, this world is not real", she might have a mouthful of things to say to you. But this is something you must understand deeply in order to practice this meditation – nothing real ever dies. This is a point many masters have made. The Essence of your loved ones lives on after their bodies pass away. The essence of anything is God. God never dies. The different parts of God only change form. Your loved ones never become extinct. They are always alive in a different form. The second point to understand is that nothing unreal ever survives. Whatever we see being destroyed is unreal. It is an illusion. It doesn't really exist. It is like watching a movie. When the movie ends, you know no one was destroyed, no one was actually killed. The Ashtavakra Gita explains all this in a beautiful way:

> *You are the Self.*
> *You are God.*
>
> *The body is confined*
> *by its natural properties.*
>
> *It comes,*
> *it stays for a while*
> *and it goes.*
>
> *But the Self neither comes nor goes.*
> *So why do you grieve for the body?*
>
> *If the body remained till the end of time,*
> *or vanished even today,*
> *what would you gain or lose?*
>
> *You are nothing but the soul.*

Verse 134 gives one particular reason why this world is unreal or void. It is not a separate meditation. The external world is dependent on knowledge. Knowledge of the world means the law of cause and effect. Because of cause and effect, there is change, there is activity. Everything in this world is dependent on cause and effect. The Real Self (God) is beyond cause and effect. It is not dependent on any cause to exist. It is the Observer. Therefore, the nature of the external world is completely different from God. Hence, it is an illusion, or it is void.

☙ 135 ❧

Neither bondage nor liberation for me. Those terrified of these concepts should see them as images of the mind, just like the image of the sun in water.

This is the ultimate understanding. When you understand this verse, you lose all your fears. Bondage and liberation are only concepts of the mind. In truth, none of them exist. We are always free, we are always a part of God. We have only forgotten our Real Identity.

Those terrified of these concepts should see them as images of the mind, just like the image of the sun in water. When you look at an image of the sun in water, the image is sometimes clear and sometimes distorted, depending on the condition of the water. If the water is still, we see a clear image of the sun. If there are ripples in the water, we see a distorted image. If the water is muddy, we may not see any image at all. If we were to form an opinion about the sun by looking at its reflection in water, we would think that the sun is something that could change, get distorted, and even be destroyed. In actual fact, the sun never gets distorted or destroyed. It remains shinning brilliantly. We think the sun gets destroyed, because we see it through water. By seeing the sun through an intermediary (water), we are getting an inaccurate picture about the sun. Similarly, by seeing ourselves through our mind (an intermediary), we get an inaccurate picture about ourselves. It is the mind that gives us a separate identity, the ego. We then think that this ego-self of ours is subject to bondage or freedom. In truth, the ego does not exist. It is something unreal, like a shadow. We are never separate, we are always a part of God. We were never bound, and we are neither liberated. We have only forgotten our true identity. To remember our true self, we need to put the mind aside. If we wanted to see the real sun, we would need to stop looking at its image in water, and look up and see the sun directly. In the same way, we need to put the mind (our ego) aside. Then, we will directly "see" our true nature.

In non-dualism, there is only God, and nothing else. There will always be only God and nothing else. What is subject to bondage and liberation? God? No, that is not possible. God is forever free. We think of ourselves as our ego, and we think that this ego is subject to bondage and liberation. In actual fact, our ego or mind-body complex is not real. We are always a part of God. Therefore, we are not bound nor liberated. We are always free.

You practice this verse by believing you are free. What you believe is what you become. When you believe and understand that you are always free, you become free. This verse also shows us that there is nothing we have to do, we are forever free. When you understand this, you fully embrace the present moment. You stop thinking about the future, and your mind falls silent. You stop thinking about the future because you realize that you are perfect and free right here, right now. The present circumstances of your life are perfect. It is not necessary to "go" anywhere, or "get" anywhere, or achieve anything. You are already wherever you wanted to go.

The irony here is that after giving us so many methods and meditations for liberation, we are now given one where we have to do nothing. In most meditation practices, we have to do something. We are at a particular stage of our evolution and we have to "get" to a place called liberated. This verse turns this logic on its head. It says there is nothing we have to do, we are already where we want to go – we are free this very moment. When you understand this truth, you forget all about the past and the future, and live in the present moment.

Verse 135 has given us a very simple and easy way to be liberated. If you understand the truth it is conveying, you may be liberated within a few minutes. However, if it does not work for you, then you will have to "do" something. You will have to practice some other meditation, or choose another path to God.

The Ashtavakra Gita expresses the same message as that of this verse in a beautiful way. It says that the body and its fears are false. Heaven and hell, freedom and bondage are all inventions of the mind. It then goes on to say:

In the ocean of existence,
there was, there is
and there will be,
only one.

There is neither bondage
nor liberation for you.

You are already fulfilled.
Live happily.

136

All contact with pleasure, pain, etc., are through the sense organs. Therefore, one should detach oneself from the senses, turn within and abide in one's own self.

This is a beautiful verse that summarizes some of the important teachings of this text. We experience pleasure, pain and other physical sensations through our sense organs. Our emotions are also influenced by whatever information we receive through the sense organs. We constantly "react" to our external environment. Certain events make us happy, and certain events make us sad. To reach God, or to realize our true nature, we have to stop external events from influencing us. In other words, we have to have control over our emotions. That is when we become a master – a master over ourselves.

Detachment from the senses is important for another reason as explained by the great sage, Patanjali, in his *Yoga Sutras*. If we keep chasing sensory pleasures, it becomes difficult to still the mind. Patanjali explained it was necessary to detach from what we are experiencing through the sense organs, in order to control the mind. He called this step, *Ptratyahara*, the fifth limb of yoga. This verse is giving us the same message.

turn within and abide in one's own self. This part of the verse is important. It summarizes the essential teaching of yoga. Redirect your attention inward. Let most of your attention be directed back towards yourself. This is the master key, and one of the most important things to learn about yoga and meditation.

Redirecting our attention within is also important for another reason. It is only within that we find abundant joy. All the joy, all the love, all the peace, all the happiness we ever desired, is within us. This is a point this text has repeated continuously Verse 15 onwards. We constantly seek happiness outside, and that is why we sometimes suffer. When external events are not to our liking, we become unhappy. But within, we have a constant source of joy or love. This internal source is not dependent on external events. It is there continuously. To experience it we have to redirect our attention there. One has to abide in one's own self, as the verse says.

To abide in one's own self means that one should constantly be self-aware. One can simply be aware of one's self, or one can be aware of one's breath. Ramana Maharshi used to emphasize being aware of the self. He used to say that if you direct your attention inwards to the self, you experience bliss. If you direct it outwards, you experience pain. He gave a beautiful example to explain how to practice this. He said, if you have a cow that strays outside her stall, you will tempt her to stay within, by giving her fine fodder and grass to eat. Initially, she may still resist, and keep straying outside her stall. Gradually, she will enjoy staying in her stall till finally, she is so happy there that even if you coax her to come out, she will refuse. The mind works in a similar way. Initially, when you focus your attention within, you will find your mind straying outwards. When this happens, you will have to keep redirecting your awareness within, to the self. Gradually, you will start enjoying the peace you experience within. Finally, a time will come when you will experience internal happiness, and then you will find that the mind no longer strays outwards.

When you are continuously aware of yourself, or your breath, your mind quietens down. You immediately feel peaceful. When the mind becomes completely silent, you feel an explosion of joy, and then your true nature is revealed. You will then fully understand that you never needed anything external to be happy or joyful. You are the source of all the joy that you were looking for outside.

Detachment from the external world or from our senses is very important. It is something all spiritual traditions emphasize. Detachment does not mean renouncing everything or running away from a particular situation. Detachment is about changing one's attitude. It is about remaining peaceful in the face of a calamity. It is about changing our inner reaction. We have no control over external events, but we certainly have control over our inner reaction to them. It becomes easier to detach from the external world, when you realize that the source of all the joy and happiness you desire is within you. That is what this verse is teaching us. Go within, reside within. That is where you will find abundant joy.

ଓ 137 ଡ

All things are revealed by the knower. The Self is revealed through all things. As their own nature is the same, perceive the knower and the known as one.

To understand this verse, consider yourself to be the subject, and everything else to be objects. You are the subject and the knower. You reveal or perceive all things. You consider yourself to have a different identity from other objects, and you give a separate identity to other objects. You call other people or other objects by their name. You define other objects, and because of you, other objects are known.

The Self is revealed through all things. This relationship works both ways. You know yourself only because of other objects. If there was no other object, how could you perceive of yourself as someone with a separate identity? You need at least one other object, so that you can define yourself in relation to that. You can define yourself as being different from that.

As their own nature is the same, perceive the knower and the known as one. Their nature is the same, because without one, the other does not exist. Because of the subject, objects are given an identity. Because of objects, the subject is given an identity.

One cannot exist without the other. Because they cannot exist separately, they cannot be separate. They are all one and the same thing. Therefore, perceive of yourself as one with everything else. Believe you are one with all of life. You are not separate with the rest of existence. Because without them, you have no meaning. When you believe you are one with all of life, you drop your ego. And then, you become one with God and all of existence.

CHAPTER 3

THE JOY

It is in fact from bliss that all beings are born.
Once born, they live by bliss and when they depart,
they merge into bliss.

—Taittiriya Upanishad

Verse 137 concludes the meditations. After this, there are further questions and answers between God and the Goddess. These questions and answers explain certain aspects of the philosophy of non-dualism.

☙ 138 ❧

Mind, intellect, energy of life and limited self. O Dear One, when this group of four disappears, then the state of God appears.

Mind, intellect, energy of life and limited self, all constitute the ego. When this group of four disappears, we reach our highest state – the state of God. This is an important point to understand about non-dualism. Union with God is not a union of two. It is a union of one. We are not separate from God. We are always one with God. To realize our Divinity, our oneness with God, we have to get rid of our ego. Our ego and God cannot exist at the same time. When our ego disappears, God appears. Conversely, when our ego is present, God is absent.

When our mind and intellect disappear, it does not mean that they have been destroyed. It only means that the mind has now come under our control. It is now a tool we can use, as and when we choose to. It no longer controls us.

Similarly, the disappearance of life energy does not mean that our body is destroyed. It means that our energy *grows* to that of the state of God.

≈ 139 ≈

O Goddess, I have described in brief a hundred and twelve meditations, by which a person can still the mind. Knowing them, a person becomes wise.

All the meditations seek to still the mind. Our uncontrolled thoughts give us a separate sense of identity. The voice that continues inside our head creates an unreal self, our ego. When the mind falls silent, our separate sense of identity disappears. We then reach a state of full awareness and joy. The state of God appears in us.

Knowing them, a person becomes wise. The main purpose of our life is to unite with God. Knowledge that helps us achieve this objective, such as knowledge of these meditations, is true wisdom. This knowledge makes one wise.

≈ 140 ≈

By being proficient in any one of these practices, a person will be united with God, and God will be born within oneself. One can then perform any work with his word alone. One will have the ability to confer malediction or benediction.

One has to be proficient in any one meditation. No meditation is superior to any other. What works for you is better for you. Some other meditation may work for someone else. There are many paths to God, and each one gets us there. Although, the verse advises that one can practice only one meditation, for faster results one should initially practice two. One should practice a sitting meditation, and a meditation during the entire day. A sitting meditation helps one still one's mind quickly. However, after the meditation is over, if we allow the mind to wander freely for the rest of the day, then most of the benefits of the meditation will be lost. Instead, one should try and remain aware throughout the day. Then, progress will be very rapid.

One can then perform any work with his word alone. We create our future reality with our thoughts, and our level of awareness. The greater the level of awareness, the faster we produce results. When we reach our highest state, we create results almost instantaneously. The time gap between our thoughts or desires, and their being transformed into reality, shrinks dramatically. It fact, it almost disappears. One produces results effortlessly. If we first chase material goods, we will have to put in effort into acquiring them. Instead, if we take the spiritual path, we can also acquire material goods, and that too effortlessly. Ironically, after making progress on the spiritual path, one will become least interested in worldly goods and pleasures. The joy obtained within is far greater than anything the external world can offer.

One will have the ability to confer malediction or benediction. One has to be careful with this verse. It can easily be misunderstood. The verse is basically trying to say that after enlightenment, one becomes powerful and is able to produce results quickly. No enlightened person confers malediction. If they do, they cannot be enlightened. If you look at the history of enlightened masters – Krishna, Buddha, Christ, Patanjali, Mahatma

Gandhi, Ramakrishna, etc. you will find that none of them deliberately tried to harm any person. There are two reasons why an enlightened person will never harm another person. An enlightened person has discovered her true nature, which is joy. She is always joyful. Her joy is not dependent on external circumstances. Only an angry person tries to harm another. A joyful person would never harm another. Even if you attacked a master, she would not get upset. She knows you are only attacking her body, and she is not her body. A master also realizes that they are one with all of life. It would therefore be foolish to confer malediction, because as per the law of karma, whatever you do to others, you will one day experience the same. Even if you harm a master, they will only respond with love, they will never try and harm you. When we are all one, it makes no sense to hurt anybody.

141

He becomes immortal and free from old age. He is endowed with the power of becoming as small as an atom, and with other powers. O Goddess, he becomes the favorite of the female yogis, and the master of spiritual gatherings. Even while living, he is liberated. Though he performs worldly activities, he is not affected by them.

Yoga says that after a certain stage of spiritual development, one is endowed with certain powers. They are eight in number, and are called the *ashta siddhis*. They are:

(1) Anima – the power of making the body as small as an atom.
(2) Laghima – the power of making the body light.
(3) Mahima – the power of making the body large.
(4) Garima – the power of making the body heavy.
(5) Prapti – the capacity to reach anywhere.
(6) Prakamya – the power of fulfilling any desire.
(7) Vashitwa – control over all objects, organic and inorganic.
(8) Ishitva – the power to create and destroy at will.

These powers are not to be used lightly. They are considered a distraction on the spiritual path. The irony here is that one gains these powers just before liberation, when the ego is virtually absent. When the ego is gone, one has no desires left, and therefore no use of these powers. It is for this reason that these powers can never be misused. They become available only when one has no ego left, and therefore no desire of harming anyone else.

Though he performs worldly activities, he is not affected by them. External events, no matter how terrible they may be, have no effect on an enlightened person. A liberated person resides in the bliss of her own nature. She is completely free of the external world. The world has no power over her.

The Goddess said:

☙ 142 ❧

O God, if this is the nature of the Supreme Energy,

☙ 143 ❧

as described, then who will one continuously recite a mantra on, and what will one recite? O Great Lord, who is to be meditated on, who is be worshipped, and who is to be gratified? To whom does one offer oblations to or perform sacrifices for, and in what way?

If God is not separate from us, and God is all there is, then who does one meditate on? Who does one pray to or perform sacrifices for? It is easier to worship God when you think God is separate from you. But what if God is not separate from you? Who do you worship then?

God said:

☙ 144 ❧

O Deer Eyed One, these practices referred to are external and only pertain to gross forms.

The practices the Goddess has referred to are external rituals. They pertain to gross forms, not to actual reality.

☙ 145 ❧

That meditation made again and again on the Supreme Being is continuous mantra recitation. One should meditate on the spontaneous sound that continues within oneself in the form of a mantra. This is what mantra chanting is really about.

The practice of mantra chanting is important in some schools of yoga. The master gives the disciple a personal mantra, based on the disciple's date and place of birth. The chanting of this personal mantra is sufficient to liberate a person. This text says here that a more effective practice is listening to the sound of one's breath. The sound of one's breath is a mantra. Listening to this sound is what mantra chanting is really about. The practice of listening to one's breath is described fully in Verses 154-156.

☙ 146 ❧

Meditation is unswerving concentration without form or support. Concentration on an imaginary figure of the Divine with body, eyes, face, hands, etc., is not meditation.

In Hinduism, images are made of the various Gods and Goddesses. Sometimes, some of these images are used to concentrate on. Lord Shiva is usually shown with long hair, sitting cross-legged, with mountains in the background. This text is against all these imaginary images of God. God has no particular form, although God can take any form or shape.

☙ 147 ❧

Offering of flowers, etc., is not called worship. One should firmly fix the heart on the Supreme Space, which is beyond thought. From that love, there is union with God. That indeed is worship.

Hinduism, at a time in history, had become excessively ritualistic. Yoga was always against rituals. External rituals are not important. It is inner change that is important. That is why offering of flowers and other rituals are not considered real worship.

One should firmly fix the heart on the Supreme Space, which is beyond thought. Because we are never separate from God, does not mean that we cannot pray or worship God. While the ego is still present, we feel separate from God. In such circumstances, it can be very helpful to pray to God, and seek God's help. What the verse is saying is, forget about external rituals. Instead, fix the heart firmly on the Supreme Space or God. The heart never lies. If you truly seek God, you will reach God. This is a very important point to understand. It is something that Patanjali emphasized in the *Yoga Sutras* – the greater your desire for reaching God, the faster you reach God. If your desire is very great, you can reach God even in a single moment. That is why the verse says, set your heart firmly on God.

The use of the term Supreme Space for God, is meant to convey the true nature of God. When we use the term God, we think of someone or something exclusive and superior to us, located at a particular place, and separate from us. However, God is not *exclusive* but *inclusive.* God is not separate from all things, but includes all things. That is why the term Supreme Space is used. Space, like God, is everywhere. It is *in* everything, and *around* everything.

148

By being established in even one of the meditations explained here, one will experience consciousness rising day after day, till one reaches the Highest State. That is known here as satisfaction.

By properly practicing any one of the meditations given here, one will experience awareness increasing day after day, till one reaches full awareness. Kashmir poetess and saint, Lalla, used to say that becoming more and more awake, was a wonderful experience.

☙ 149 ❧

When the organs of sense, objects of sense, etc., are offered along with the mind, to be dissolved in the fire of the Supreme Void, with consciousness as a ladle – that is real oblation.

Lalla used to teach that our greatest offering to God was our increasing awareness. That is similar to what this verse is saying. The best offering we can make to God is to dissolve our ego, and reach our highest state – the state of God. This is done by controlling the mind and detaching from objects of sense.

Supreme Void is the term used for God in this verse. It is meant to convey that God is everything. If God is everything, then God is also nothing. Not a particular thing, but everything. This is the meaning of void in this verse.

☙ 150 ❧

O Parvati, from destroying all of one's sins, one is completely absorbed into the Supreme Being, and obtains satisfaction described as bliss. This is the meaning of sacrifice in this system.

Destroying all of one's sins, means destroying one's ego. One sacrifices one's ego. That is the meaning of sacrifice in this system. When the ego is destroyed, one is absorbed into God and obtains bliss.

☙ 151 ❧

The union of God and Energy. That Supreme State should be one's place of pilgrimage. Otherwise, in one's true state, who will worship and who will one satisfy?

The union of God and Energy, refers to the union of the individual with God. Energy stands for the individual. People go on pilgrimages to various places. It is always interesting to visit places where the great saints lived. Some of these places have a sense of peace and tranquility, long after these saints have passed away. This verse emphasizes meeting God, uniting with God. That is the best place of pilgrimage. We meet God within. Therefore, the best place to go on a pilgrimage, is within. Like some of the previous verses, this verse emphasizes the internal over the external. Lalla summed it up best when she said, "I made pilgrimages, looking for God. Then I gave up, turned around, there God was inside me!"

Otherwise, in one's true state, who will worship and who will one satisfy? This philosophy does not encourage external forms of worship. In one's true state there is only One. The worshipper and the worshipped are not separate. Therefore, who is there to worship? There is only you. There is only One. There is only God.

☙ 152 ❧

The essence of one's Self consists entirely of freedom, bliss and consciousness. Immersing our limited self into our True Self, is bathing.

God's essence consists of freedom, bliss and consciousness. Since we are a part of God, our essence is also freedom, bliss and consciousness. People always long to be free. You will notice this most with nations. People who live in countries that are run by totalitarian regimes, will always resist and struggle to be free. It does not matter whether the country is communist or a religious fundamentalist society. The ideology does not matter, the lack of freedom does. People will always rebel against the lack of freedom, because freedom is the essence of who they are. Parents often discover this with their children. Beyond a certain age children like to be free, and resist being dominated by their parents. The material world is also constructed on a similar principle. Economies that are free and open, tend to develop faster than closed economies.

People sometimes ask that if our essence consists of joy or bliss, why do we not always feel blissful. The answer has to do with the mind. As long as the mind is uncontrolled and continues its inner chatter, we do not feel blissful. When the mind falls silent, we experience the bliss of our true nature.

Immersing our limited self into our True Self, is bathing. In certain rituals, bathing is required as a first step towards purification. In this philosophy, bathing consists of dissolving our ego into our True Self. In external rituals, we purify our body through bathing. Bathing or purification here means to dissolve the ego. The ego is like a layer of dirt covering our True Self. We bathe by dissolving this covering, thereby allowing our True Self to emerge.

☙ 153 ❧

The objects with which worship is to be done, or with which the Higher and Lower Reality is to be satisfied, the worshipper, and God are in fact all one and the same. Why then, this worship?

The non-dualistic philosophy of this text discourages ritualistic and external forms of worship. The worshipper, the objects used for worship, and God are all one and the same. So who is worshipping whom? You are in fact worshipping yourself, using yourself (objects of worship). This tradition found all this pointless. Why waste your time in these futile rituals? Instead, seek to transform yourself and realize your Divine Nature, by practicing the meditations given in this text.

☙ 154 ❧

The breath goes out and the breath comes in spontaneously, in a curved manner. She reaches far, higher and lower. The Great Goddess is the supreme place of pilgrimage.

There is one final meditation now being given, which is described in this, and the next three verses. The Great Goddess is the breath. She is the supreme place of pilgrimage. This means, one should visit her – one should focus one's attention on one's breath.

☙ 155 ❧

This fire (Goddess) is full of Great Bliss. By following her and resting in her, one becomes fully identified with her. Then, through the Goddess, one obtains God.

The fire referred to in this text is the breath. The breath is full of great bliss. One has to follow the breath – continuously remain aware of the breath. Then one becomes identified with her, and one becomes blissful. After that, one reaches God.

☙ 155(a) ❧

The breath makes the sound Sa when it goes outside, and again makes the sound Ha when it enters inside. "Hamsa, Hamsa." This mantra is continuously recited by a living being.

ꕥ 156 ꕥ

21,600 times during a day and night. This continuous recitation of the Goddess fully described, is easy to attain. It is difficult only for the senseless.

Verse 155a is not given in the Kashmir Series of Texts and Studies. However, it was part of the original text, as it has been quoted by Ksemaraja in his commentary of the *Shiva Sutras*. It is important because it explains the meditation. Without it, Verse 156 would make no sense as Verse 155a ends in mid sentence and Verse 156 continues from there. It has been given the number 155a, so as not to disturb the numbering of verses given in the Kashmir Series of Texts and Studies.

The meditation practice is to listen to the sound of one's breath. It can be practiced throughout the day, or as a sitting meditation with eyes closed. The breath makes the sound *Ham* when it enters, and makes the sound *Sa* when it goes outside. *Ham* comes from the Sanskrit word *aham* which means I. *Sa* means that. Therefore, *Hamsa* means I am That. That stands for Shiva or God. The breath continuously makes the sound I am That or I am God, 15 times a minute (we breathe in and out approximately 15 times a minute), or 21,600 times in 24 hours. This sound is considered to be a mantra. It is one of the most important mantras for raising consciousness.

Ham is pronounced Hum. Therefore one should hear the sound Hum while breathing in and Sa while breathing out. More commonly, the sound is reversed. One hears the sound So (not Sa) while breathing in, and the sound Hum while breathing out. The meaning is the same. You will have to experiment to find out what sound your breath makes. It may be Hum while breathing in and Sa while breathing out. Or it may be So while breathing in and Hum while breathing out. Or it may also be something else.

To practice this meditation, sit comfortably and close your eyes. Focus your attention on the sound of your breath, whether it is Humsa, Sohum or some other sound. Continue to remain aware of this sound. You will find yourself going very deep and becoming very peaceful.

Why has this practice been described now and not with the other meditations? That is because this meditation is special. It is easy to do and always succeeds in stilling the mind. If all other meditations fail, this one will always succeed. It works for everyone. The sound of one's breath is the most powerful mantra in the whole universe. It is the basic mantra of life and God. It has a very powerful effect on the mind. The mind is attracted to this sound, and listening to it, falls silent. All thoughts end, and one experiences the peace and joy of one's true nature.

This continuous recitation of the Goddess fully described, is easy to attain. You can substitute the word breath for Goddess, and then you will find the sentence easier to understand.

It is difficult only for the senseless. The word senseless is to be taken literally. This practice is difficult only for those who are senseless – who have fainted, or are unconscious for some reason. For everyone else who is awake, conscious, or in their senses, this practice is easy. It works for everyone.

ꕥ 157 ꕥ

O Goddess, with these words, I have explained the supreme teaching, which leads one to the highest state of immortality. This teaching should not be revealed to just anyone.

ꕥ 158 ꕥ

Particularly to pupils of another tradition, or pupils who are wicked, cruel, and unfaithful to their master. On the contrary, it may be fearlessly given to the brave ones, whose minds are free of doubts,

These two verses should be read along with the first sentence of Verse 159. There are a few conditions a person must fulfill, before they are eligible to learn these meditations. A pupil should not belong to another tradition. If she does, then she will have doubts, and will not be fully committed to this path. Then progress will be very slow or nonexistent. A master has to teach a pupil who has no doubts, and is fully committed, and faithful to the master. Being faithful or devoted to your master is important. If you do not believe in your master, then how can you learn what he or she has to teach you? Therefore, a student must have faith in her master. Only then will she believe and practice what the master teaches her. To teach a student who has doubts, or no faith in the master is a waste of time. Such students will make little progress.

In addition, a pupil should not be wicked or cruel. Earlier, yoga used to place a lot of emphasis on non-violence. Before a person was taught yoga, they first had to become non-violent. They were not to harm or injure other living beings. This is not a condition that is applied today. Yoga is now open to almost everyone. This is because yoga and meditation have the ability to transform one's nature. If a person is violent, meditation can make them non-violent. If a person is cruel, meditation can make them kind. Presently, meditation is also taught in jails. It helps people overcome their anger and makes them peaceful. When they are peaceful within, they will be peaceful with the outside world.

☙ 159 ❧

and who are devoted to their line of masters. One's race, government, city, country, children, wife and family –

☙ 160 ❧

One should give all this up, O Deer Eyed One. What is the point in these temporary things? Instead, O Goddess, one should seize this teaching, which leads to the everlasting, supreme treasure.

We normally define ourselves by our race, nationality, religion, or some other identity that society gives us. We are actually none of that. We are not Indian, or Chinese, or American, or anything else. Nor are we Hindu, Muslim or Christian. As we approach death, all these identities we have given ourselves, start being removed. It is important to remove these identities ourselves. We are not our body, nor any of the things by which we define our external appearance.

One's race, government, city, country, children, wife and family – One should give all this up. Giving up one's wife or children, does not mean that one should leave them and retire to the forest to meditate. People who are dependent on you should continue to be helped, till they become independent. Giving them up means one should give up attachment for them. One should love all of mankind, not just our immediate family. Also our wealth and our family are temporary. In a few days, they are all gone. The Ashtavakra Gita says that life after life we strive for wealth, only to lose it all. We keep striving for different pleasures only to lose them all when we die. What is the point in all this? In our next life, we will have to start acquiring wealth all over again. We will have to learn a language, and go through school again. Instead, we should rearrange our priorities. We should concentrate on what is permanent, not what is temporary. That is what the next part of the verse tells us.

Instead, O Goddess, one should seize this teaching, which leads to the everlasting, supreme treasure. Worldly goods, and wealth that we acquire, may be lost in one's lifetime. If they are not lost in one's lifetime, they will be lost at the time of one's death. However, this teaching leads to everlasting treasure. Even if one does not get liberated in this lifetime, the progress one makes, the level of awareness one reaches is never lost. We start our next lifetime from the level of awareness we reach in this lifetime. There is no falling down or starting again from zero. One reaches a certain level of awareness, and from there rises to higher and higher levels of awareness, till one is liberated. The progress one makes in the material world is temporary. It is lost at the time of one's death. In contrast, the progress made in the spiritual path is permanent. It continues life after life, till one reaches God.

This teaching leads to our liberation, which is the supreme treasure.

᪥ 161 ᪥

Life may even be renounced, but this teaching which leads to the supreme nectar of immortality, should not be given to undeserving ones.

The Goddess said:

O God, O God of Gods, O Great God,
I am completely satisfied.

162

I have now fully understood the essence of the Rudrayamala Tantra, and the essence of the different grades of Energy.

The *Vigyan Bhairava Tantra* was believed to be part of a text called the Rudrayamala Tantra. However, the Goddess here is referring to all texts of tantra that deal with the subject of Rudrayamala, or liberation. The essence of all these texts on liberation, is this dialogue – the *Vigyan Bhairava Tantra.*

163

Having said these words, the Goddess who was filled with joy, then embraced God.

The Goddess was filled with joy because all her doubts had been removed. She embraced God in the sense that she became one with God – She returned to Her highest non-dual state. She had separated Herself to show all of mankind how to return to God. Now that the task had been completed, she returned to Her highest state.

CONCLUSION

There are many meditations given in the text. Any one meditation is sufficient to take one to God. However, the speed with which one reaches God depends on the intensity of one's desire. The greater the desire, the faster one returns to their Highest State.

The philosophy of monism or non-dualism has become increasingly popular in the last 150 years. There are many messengers and enlightened saints who are teaching this philosophy, or have taught it in the recent past. They include Neale Donald Walsch, Ramakrishna, Eckhart Tolle, Osho, Ramana Maharshi, Swami Vivekananda, Adi Shankara, Swami Sivananda, Sai Baba, Paramahansa Yogananda, Deepak Chopra, Wayne W. Dyer, and many others. Their books are a good source for learning more about the philosophy of non-dualism. Amongst ancient texts, the other important ones are the Upanishads, the Shiva Sutras, the Yoga Sutras and the Ashtavakra Gita.

Over the last century, mankind has made tremendous spiritual progress. We are beginning to move away from the narrow divisions created by religions and society, towards a higher truth. As we evolve, we are helped on our way by messengers of God, enlightened saints, and texts like the

Vigyan Bhairava Tantra, that were hidden for centuries. Important ancient texts like the Vigyan Bhairava Tantra, reappear at just the right time - when we are ready to receive its message and move forward in our evolution. One has to be grateful to the enlightened Kashmir Master who this text was revealed to. He (or She) did not leave his name behind because he knew that names are not important. Instead, he left us something far more valuable. He showed us many, many ways to be enlightened. To him or to her, we remain grateful.

Ranjit Chaudhri
Kolkata

BIBLIOGRAPHY

Bancroft, Anne. *The Buddha Speaks.* Boston: Shambhala, 2000.

Barks, Coleman. *Lalla – Naked Song.* Athens, GA: Maypop Books, 1992.

Burtt, E.A. *The Teachings of the Compassionate Buddha.* New York: New American Library, 1955, 1982.

Byrom, Thomas. *The Heart of Awareness – A Translation of the Ashtavakra Gita.* Boston: Shambhala, 1990, 2001.

Harding, D.E. *On Having No Head.* London: Arkana Penguin Books Ltd, 1986.

Katie, Byron. *Loving What Is - Four questions that can change your life.* New York: Three Rivers Press, 2002, 2003.

Kaul, Rakesh K. *The last Queen of Kashmir.* India: Harper Collins Publishers India, 2016, 2020.

Lakshmanjoo, Swami. *Kashmir Shaivism, The Secret Supreme.* USA: Kashmir Shaivism Fellowship, 1985, 2000.

Maharshi, Sri Ramana. *Words Of Grace.* Tiruvannamalai: Sri Ramanasramam, 1969, 1996.

Mascaro, Juan. *The Bhagavad Gita.* England: Penguin Books Ltd, 1962, 1975.

Mascaro, Juan. *The Upanishads.* England: Penguin Books Ltd, 1965, 1981.

Mukherjee, Radhakamal. *Astavakragita* (The Song of the Self Supreme). India: Motilal Banarsidass Publishers Private Limited, 1971, 2000.

Osho. *The Book of Secrets.* New York: St. Martin's Griffin, 1998.

Osho. *Enlightenment: The Only Revolution – Discourses on the great mystic Ashtavakra.* Pune: The Rebel Publishing House Pvt. Ltd., 1998, 1999.

Osho. *Osho Meditation Series – Surrender to Existence.* Delhi: FULL CIRCLE, 1997.

Radhakrishnan, S. *The Principal Upanishads.* India: Harper Collins Publishers India, 1994, 1997.

Reps, Paul and Senzaki, Nyogen. *Zen Flesh, Zen Bones.* Boston: Shambhala, 1957, 1994.

Silburn, Lilian. *Kundalini – energy of the depths.* Albany, NY: State University of New York Press, 1988.

Singh, Jaideva. *Vijnana Bhairava or Divine Consciousness.* Delhi: Motilal Banarsidass Publishers Private Limited, 1979, 2001.

Singh, Jaideva. *Siva Sutras.* Delhi: Motilal Banarsidass Publishers Private Limited, 1979, 2000

Tolle, Eckhart. *The Power of Now.* Mumbai: Yogi Impressions, 1997, 2001.

Venkataramiah, Mungala. *Talks with Sri Ramana Maharshi.* Tiruvannamalai: Sri Ramanasramam, 1955, 2000.

Walsch, Neale Donald. *Conversations With God Book 1, an uncommon dialogue.* Great Britain: Hodder and Stoughton, 1997.

Walsch, Neale Donald. *Friendship With God, An uncommon dialogue.* Great Britain: Hodder and Stoughton, 1999.

Walsch, Neale Donald. *Communion with God, An uncommon dialogue.* Great Britain: Hodder and Stoughton, 2000.

Yogananda, Sri Sri Paramahansa. *God Talks With Arjuna: The Bhagavad Gita.* Kolkata: Yogoda Satsanga Society of India, 2002.

Yogananda, Sri Sri Paramhansa. *Journey To Self-Realization, Collected Talks, Volume III.* Kolkata: Yogoda Satsanga Society of India, 2001.

--------. *The Holy Bible, King James Version.* New York: New American Library, 1974.

GUIDELINES FOR SITTING MEDITATIONS

a) It is best to learn a sitting meditation under the guidance of a master. Some sitting meditations are very powerful and can even harm one, if practiced incorrectly. Three meditations that are perfectly safe to practice are – chanting AUM (verses 39 and 42) and listening to the sound of one's breath (verses 155-156).

b) One should sit in a relaxed, comfortable posture, without any tension whatsoever. One should sit on a mat, towel or blanket, placed on the floor or on a carpet. The best postures for meditation are *ardha siddhasana, padmasana* (lotus posture), and *siddhasana.* The next best are *swastikasana, ardha padmasana, sukhasana,* and *vajrasana.* These can be learnt from a good yoga teacher. Some people may not be able to initially sit in these postures. They may need to improve the flexibility of their body by practicing other yoga postures, or other forms of exercise. If, for some reason, a person cannot maintain any of the above postures, then the meditation can be done sitting in any other posture one feels comfortable in. It can even be done sitting on a chair. Unless specified, meditation should not be practiced lying down. While lying down, there is a tendency to drift into sleep.

c) During the meditation practice, the body should be kept motionless, and the spine should be kept straight. The postures mentioned above are useful, as they lock the body into a fixed position, and keep the spine erect. Moving the body while practicing meditation is a distraction. It prevents one from going deep into the practice. Generally, this is not a problem. Once a person starts a meditation, they automatically get absorbed into the practice. After completing the practice, externalize your awareness slowly. For example, one can first place their attention on the breath. Then, become aware of the body, specially the contact between the body and the floor. Next become aware of sounds in the external environment. Finally, open the eyes and move the body.

d) The best time for practice is between 4 and 6 a.m. The next best time is in the evening, at dusk. Meditation can also be practiced at any other time, even before going to sleep. However, one should try and practice at the same time everyday.

e) It is best to practice meditation on an empty stomach. One should avoid practicing immediately after a heavy meal. When the digestive system is working, it becomes a distraction and affects the practice.

f) Wear loose, light and comfortable clothing. Practice in a quiet, clean environment. Excessive external noise is a distraction during meditation.

g) Generally, a sitting meditation should be practiced twice a day, for 15 minutes at a time. For longer periods, it is necessary to practice only under the guidance of a master. There is no substitute to learning meditation from a competent teacher.

h) Practice every day. This is most important. No matter what your lifestyle or how often one has to travel, one must find some time every day to practice meditation. Otherwise, progress will be slow.

i) In case of illness or fever, one should temporarily stop the practice. Restart once health improves.

THE VERSES

Śrī devy uvāca

The Goddess said:

1) **Śrutaṃ deva mayā sarvaṃ rudrayāmalasambhavam |**
Trikabhedam aśeṣeṇa sārāt sāravibhāgaśaḥ | |
Adyāpi na nivṛtto me saṃśayaḥ parameśvara |
I have heard everything originating from the union of God and the Goddess. From the essence of the Trika System, along with its subdivisions. But, O God, even now my doubts have not been removed.

2) **Kiṃ rūpaṃ tattvato deva śabdarāśikalāmayam | |**
O God, what is your real nature? Is it a collection of words?

3) **Kiṃ vā navātmabhedena bhairave bhairavākṛtau |**
Triśirobhedabhinnaṃ vā kiṃ vā śaktitrayātmakam | |
Or does the nature of God consist of nine different forms? Or is it a combination of three different heads, or three energies?

4) **Nādabindumayaṃ vāpi kiṃ candrārdhanirodhikāḥ |**
Cakrārūḍham anackaṃ vā kiṃ vā śaktisvarūpakam | |
Or are you consisting of sound, or point, or half moon? Is your nature that of energy ascending the chakras, or is it the voweless sound?

5) **Parāparāyāḥ sakalam aparāyāśca vā punaḥ |**
Parāyā yadi tadvat syāt paratvaṃ tad virudhyate | |
Is medium and inferior energy divisible in parts? If that is also the nature of supreme (transcendent) energy, then it is inconsistent with transcendence.

6) **Nahi varṇvibhedena dehabhedena vā bhavet |**
Paratvaṃ niṣkalatvena, sakalatve na tad bhavet | |
Prasādaṃ kuru me nātha niḥśeṣaṃ chindhi saṃśayam | |
The Supreme Being is certainly not a division of color or bodies. How can the Supreme Being be indivisible and yet be a composite of parts? O Lord, be gracious on me, and remove my doubts completely.

Bhairava uvāca
God said:

7) **Sādhu sādhu tvayā pṛṣṭaṃ tantrasāram idam priye | |**
Excellent! Excellent! Dear one, you have asked the essence of tantra.

8) **Gūhanīyatamaṃ bhadre tathāpi kathayāmi te |**
Yatkiñcit saklaṃ rūpam bhairavasya prakīrtitam | |
Dear one, even though the subject is very difficult to understand, I will explain it to you. Whatever has been declared as the divisible forms of God –

9) **Tad asāratayā devi vijñeyaṃ śakrajālavat |**
Māyāsvapnopamaṃ caiva gandharvanagarabhramam | |

Know that O Goddess to be insubstantial, like a magic show, or like an illusory dream, or as an imaginary city in the sky.

10) **Dhyānārthaṃ bhrāntabuddhīnāṃ kriyāḍambaravartinām |**
Kevalaṃ varṇitam puṃsāṃ vikalpanihatātmanām | |
These concepts are used as a support for meditation for people of confused minds, who are interested in performing external actions. It is only for those people who are stuck in dualizing thoughts.

11) **Tattvato na navātmāsau śabdarāśir na bhairavaḥ |**
Na cāsau triśirā devo na ca śaktitrayātmakaḥ | |
In reality, God is neither of nine different forms nor a collection of words. Not of three heads and nor of three energies.

12) **Nādabindumayo vāpi na candrārdhnirodhikāḥ |**
Na cakrakramasaṃbhinno na ca śaktisvarūpakaḥ | |
Not sound or point, nor half moon. Ascending the chakras is not my essence, and nor is energy my nature.

13) **Aprabuddhamatīnāṃ hi etā bālavibhīṣikāḥ |**
Mātṛmodakavatsarvaṃ pravṛttyarthaṃ udāhṛtam | |
These concepts are for those whose intellect is not mature enough to understand Ultimate Reality. They are just like a mother who frightens children away from danger, and encourages everyone to commence their spiritual practices.

14) **Dikkālakalanonmuktā deśoddeśāviśeṣiṇī |**
Vyapadeṣṭum aśakyāsāv akathyā paramārthataḥ | |
I am free of all concepts of time or direction. I am not at a particular place. It is impossible to accurately represent or describe God in words.

15) **Antaḥ svānubhavānandā vikalponmuktagocarā |**
Yāyasthā bharitākārā bhairavī bhairavātmanaḥ | |
One may experience the joy of God within oneself, when the mind is still and free of thoughts. That state of God full of bliss, is the Goddess.

16) **Tad vapus tattvato jñeyaṃ vimalaṃ viśvapūraṇam |**
Evaṃvidhe pare tattve kaḥ pūjyaḥ kaśca tṛpyati | |
One should know my essential nature to be that joy, pure, and pervading the entire universe. As this is the nature of the Supreme Reality, who is to be worshipped and who is to be satisfied?

17) **Evaṃvidhā bhairavasya yāvasthā parigīyate |**
Sā parā pararūpeṇa parā devī prakīrtitā | |
In this way, God's highest state is celebrated. Through that highest form of mine, the highest form of the Supreme Goddess is also being celebrated.

18) **Śakti-śaktimator yadvat abhedaḥ sarvadā sthitaḥ |**
Atas taddharmadharmitvāt parā śaktiḥ parātmanaḥ | |
No difference ever exists between energy and the possessor of energy, between duty and being dutiful.

For this reason, there is no difference between Supreme Energy (Goddess) and God.

19) **Na vahner dāhikā śaktiḥ vyatiriktā vibhāvyate |**
Kevalaṃ jñānasattāyāṃ prārambho 'yam praveśane | |
The burning power of fire cannot be considered separate from fire. It is only described separately in the beginning, to enable one to learn its essential nature.

20) **Śaktyavasthāpraviṣṭasya nirvibhāgena bhāvanā |**
Tadāsau Śivarūpī syāt śaivī mukham ihocyate | |
When one has entered the state of Divine Energy, one is in the state of God. For it is stated here that the Goddess is the entrance to God.

21) **Yathālokena dīpasya kiraṇair bhāskarasya ca |**
Jñāyate digvibhāgādi tadvac chaktyā Śivaḥ priye | |
Just as, by the light of a lamp and the rays of the sun, portions of space, etc., are perceived. Similarly, O Dear One, through the Goddess (Energy), God is known.

Śrī devy uvāca
The Goddess said:

22) **Devadeva triśūlāṅka kapālakṛtabhūṣaṇa |**
Digdeśakālaśūnyā ca vyapadeśavivarjitā | |
O God of Gods, having a cup as an ornament and a trident as an emblem, devoid of direction, place, time and description.

23) **Yāvasthā bharitākārā bhairavasyopalabhyate |**
Kair upāyair mukhaṃ tasya parā devī katham bhavhavet | |
Yathā samyag ahaṃ vedmi tathā me brūhi Bhairava |
By what means can one acquire and be filled with that form of God? In what way is the Supreme Goddess, the entrance to God? O God, explain it to me in such a manner, that I may understand it fully.

Śrī bhairava uvāca
God said:

24) **Ūrdhve prāṇo hy adho jīvo visargātmā paroccaret |**
Utpattidvitayasthāne bharaṇād bharitā sthitiḥ | |
The Supreme Energy (breath) goes upwards with exhalation and downwards with inhalation. By concentrating on the two places of its origin, one acquires the state of fulfillment.

25) **Maruto 'ntar bahir vāpi viyadyugmānivartanāt |**
Bhairavyā bhairavasyetthaṃ bhairavi vyajyate vapuḥ | |
Concentrate on the two places where the breath turns from inside to outside and also from outside to inside. O Goddess, in this way, through the Goddess, the essential form of God is realized.

26) **Na vrajen na viśec chaktir marudrūpā vikāsite |**
Nirvikalpatayā madhye tayā bhairavarūpatā | |
At the Center where the breath does not enter or the breath does not go out, all thoughts disappear. The form

of Energy becomes visible, and through her the form of God appears.

27) **Kumbhitā recitā vāpi pūritā vā yadā bhavet |**
Tadante śāntanāmāsau śaktyā śantaḥ prakāśate | |
When by itself the breath is retained after inhalation or exhalation – then in the end, through Energy known as peace, Peace is revealed.

28) **Āmūlāt kiraṇābhāsāṃ sūkṣmātsūkṣmatarātmikāṃ |**
Cintayet tāṃ dviṣaṭkānte śyāmyantīm Bhairavodayaḥ | |
Meditate on the energy in the form of a bright ray of light, rising from the root energy center, becoming subtler and subtler, until finally dissolving at the highest center. Then God appears.

29) **Udgacchantīṃ taḍidrūpām praticakraṃ kramāt kramam |**
Ūrdhvaṃ muṣṭitrayaṃ yāvat tāvad ante mahodayaḥ | |
Meditate on the energy in the form of lightning, ascending from energy center to energy center till the highest center. In the end, experience Great Love rising.

30) **Kramadvādaśakaṃ samyag dvādaśākṣarabheditaṃ |**
Sthūlasūkṣmaparasthityā muktvā muktvāntataḥ Śivaḥ | |
Meditate successively on the twelve Sanskrit letters. First in a gross form. Then leaving that aside, in a subtle form. Then leaving that aside, in a supreme form. Finally leaving them aside, become Shiva.

31) **Tayāpūryāśu mūrdhāntaṃ bhaṅktvā bhrūkṣepasetunā |**
Nirvikalpaṃ manaḥ kṛtvā sarvordhve sarvagodgamaḥ | |
Concentrate without thoughts on a point between and just above the eyebrows. The Divine Energy breaks out and rises above to the crown of the head, immediately filling one completely with her ecstasy.

32) **Śikhipakṣaiś citrarūpair maṇḍalaiḥ śūnyapañcakam |**
Dhyāyato 'nuttare śūnye praveśo hṛdaye bhavet | |
Meditate on the five voids in the form of the five colored circles on a peacock's tail. When the circles dissolve, one will enter into the Supreme Void within.

33) **Idṛśena krameṇaiva yatrakutrāpi cintanā |**
Śūnye kuḍye pare pātre svayaṃ līnā varapradā | |
Similarly, by gradually focusing one's attention on anything, whether on space, or a wall, or a great person, one is completely absorbed into the Supreme Reality.

34) **Kapālāntarmano nyasya tiṣṭhan mīlitalocanaḥ |**
Krameṇa manaso dārḍhyāt lakṣayel lakṣyam uttamam | |
Seated with eyes closed, fix one's attention inside the skull. From firmness in concentration, one will gradually perceive the Supreme Reality.

35) **Madhyanāḍī madhyasaṃsthā bisasūtrābharūpayā |**
Dhyātāntarvyomayā devyā tayā devaḥ prakāśate | |
The central channel located in the middle of the spinal

cord has the appearance of the lotus thread. Meditate on its inner space. The Goddess then reveals God.

36) **Kararuddhadṛgastreṇa bhrūbhedād dvārarodhanāt |**
Dṛṣṭe bindau kramāl līne tanmadhye paramā sthitiḥ | |
By concentrating on a point between the eyebrows, a light will be seen. Then, with the fingers of the hand, close the seven openings of the senses in the head. The light will gradually dissolve, and one will then permanently reside in their highest state.

37) **Dhāmāntaḥ-kṣobhasaṃbhūtasūkṣmāgnitilakākṛtim |**
Binduṃ śikhānte hṛdaye layante dhyāyato layaḥ | |
Press the eyes gently. A subtle light resembling a dot will appear at the top of the head, or in the heart. Absorb oneself there. From this meditation, one is absorbed into the Highest Reality.

38) **Anāhate pātrakarṇe 'bhagnaśabde sariddrute |**
Śabdabrahmaṇi niṣṇātaḥ param brahmādhigacchati | |
Bathe deeply in the continuous sound of a river flowing, or by closing the ears, hear the unstruck sound of God. One will then realize God.

39) **Praṇavādisamuccārāt plutānte śūnyabhāvanāt |**
Śūnyayā parayā śaktyā śūnyatām eti bhairavi | |
O Goddess, chant AUM, etc., slowly. Concentrate on the void at the end of the protracted sound. Then with the supreme energy of the void, one goes to the Void.

40) **Yasya kasyāpi varṇasya pūrvāntāv anubhāvayet |**
Śūnyayā śūnyabhūto 'sau śūnyākāraḥ pumān bhavet | |
Concentrate on the void at the beginning or end of the sound of any letter. Then by the power of that void, one will become the Void.

41) **Tantryādivādyaśabdeṣu dīrgheṣu kramasaṃsthiteḥ |**
Ananyacetāḥ pratyante paravyomavapur bhavet | |
Listen with undivided attention, towards the end of prolonged sounds of stringed and other musical instruments. By staying with the gradual diminishment of the sound, one will obtain the form of the Supreme Space.

42) **Piṇḍamantrasya sarvasya sthūlavarṇakrameṇa tu |**
Ardhendubindunādāntaḥśūnyoccārād bhavec chivaḥ | |
Chant AUM audibly. Gradually the sound diminishes. By concentrating on the point where the sound ends into the void, one becomes Shiva.

43) **Nijadehe sarvadikkaṃ yugapad bhāvayed viyat |**
Nirvikalpamanās tasya viyat sarvaṃ pravartate | |
With mind free of thoughts, concentrate on one's body. Imagine space simultaneously pervading in all directions. One will then become all pervasive.

44) **Pṛṣṭhaśūnyaṃ mūlaśūnyaṃ yugapad bhāvayec ca yaḥ |**
Śarīranirapekṣiṇyā śaktyā śūnyamanā bhavet | |
Meditate simultaneously, on the above as void and the

base as void. The Energy that is independent of the body will make one devoid of thoughts.

45) **Pṛṣṭhaśūnyaṃ mūlaśūnyaṃ hṛcchūnyaṃ bhāvayet sthiram |**
Yugapan nirvikalpatvānnirvikalpodayas tataḥ | |
Meditate firmly and simultaneously on the above as void, the base as void and the heart as void. Then, by being free of thoughts, will arise the state that is permanently free of thoughts.

46) **Tanūdeśe śūnyataiva kṣaṇamātraṃ vibhāvayet |**
Nirvikalpaṃ nirvikalpo nirvikalpasvarūpabhāk | |
Free of thoughts, consider for a short while, any part of one's body as only void. One becomes permanently free of thoughts. Then, one's own form attains the splendor of the state that is free of thoughts.

47) **Sarvaṃ dehagataṃ dravyaṃ viyadvyāptaṃ mṛgekṣaṇe |**
Vibhāvayet tatas tasya bhāvanā sā sthirā bhavet | |
O Deer eyed one, consider all the constituents of one's body to be pervaded by empty space. Then, one will permanently become settled in that conception.

48) **Dehāntare tvagvibhāgaṃ bhittibhūtaṃ vicintayet |**
Na Kiñcid antare tasya dhyāyann adhyeyabhāg bhavet | |
Consider the skin to be the wall of an empty body with nothing inside. By meditating like this, one reaches a place beyond meditation.

49) **Hṛdyākāśe nilīnākṣaḥ padmasampuṭamadhyagaḥ |**
Ananyacetāḥ subhage paraṃ saubhāgyam āpnuyāt | |
When the senses are absorbed in the inner space of the heart, one should concentrate with undivided attention on the center of the two bowls of the lotus, located there. Then O Beloved, one obtains the Supreme Fortune.

50) **Sarvataḥ svaśarīrasya dvādaśānte manolayāt |**
Dṛḍhabuddher dṛḍhībhūtaṃ tattvalakṣyaṃ pravartate | |
Absorb the mind completely at the end of twelve, within one's own body. When steadiness of intellect is firmly established, one's true nature is perceived.

51) **Yathā tathā yatra tatra dvādaśānte manaḥ kṣipet |**
Pratikṣaṇaṃ kṣīṇavṛtter vailakṣaṇyaṃ dinair bhavet | |
During every moment, in whatever way, in whatever place, one should fix one's attention at the end of twelve. The mind will be deprived of support and within a few days, one will be extraordinary.

52) **Kālāgninā kālapadād utthitena svakaṃ puraṃ |**
Pluṣṭaṃ vicintayed ante śāntābhāsas tadā bhavet | |
Imagine one's own body being burnt by a destructive fire, rising from the right foot, to the top. Then one will attain a calm splendor.

53) **Evam eva jagat sarvaṃ dagdhaṃ dhyātvā vikalpataḥ |**
Ananyacetasaḥ puṃsaḥ puṃbhāvaḥ paramo bhavet | |
Similarly, meditate with undivided attention, that the

entire world is burnt by fire. That person then attains the highest state.

54) **Svadehe jagato vāpi sūkṣmasūkṣmatarāṇī ca |**
Tattvāni yāni nilayaṃ dhyātvānte vyajyate parā | |
Meditate that the constitutive elements of one's own body, or the world are becoming subtle and more subtle, until they finally disappear. In the end, the Supreme Goddess is revealed.

55) **Pīnāṃ ca durbalāṃ śaktiṃ dhyātvā dvādaśagocare |**
Praviśya hṛdaye dhyāyanmuktaḥ svātantryam āpnuyāt | |
Having entered into the heart and meditated upon the energy that is gross and subtle, abiding in the twelfth, the meditator obtains freedom and liberation.

56) **Bhuvanādhvādirupeṇa cintayet kramaśo 'khilam |**
Sthūlasūkṣmaparasthityā yāvadante manolayaḥ | |
Consider the form of the entire universe being dissolved successively from the gross state to the subtle, and from the subtle state to the supreme, until finally one's mind is dissolved.

57) **Bhuvanādhvādirupeṇa cintayet kramaśo 'khilam |**
Sthūlasūkṣmaparasthityā yāvadante manolayaḥ | |
Meditate that this entire universe all round upto its end limits, is part of Shiva. By meditating in this manner – the Great Awakening.

58) **Viśvam etan mahādevi śūnyabhūtaṃ vicintayet |**
Tatraiva ca mano līnaṃ tatas tallayabhājanam | |
O Great Goddess, one should consider this entire universe to be a void. Then the mind will dissolve and one will be absorbed into the Void.

59) **Ghaṭādibhājane dṛṣṭiṃ bhittīs tyaktvā vinikṣipet |**
Tallayaṃ tatkṣaṇād gatvā tallayāt tanmayo bhavet | |
Look at a bowl or any other vessel, without seeing its partitions. From the moment one is absorbed into space, one will be full of space.

60) **Nirvṛkṣagiribhittyādideśe dṛṣṭiṃ vinikṣipet |**
Vilīne mānase bhāve vṛttikṣīṇaḥ prajāyate | |
Cast one's sight on a vast open place, with no trees, mountains, walls, etc. When one's mind has completely dissolved, one is born anew.

61) **Ubhayor bhāvayor jñāne dhyātvā madhyaṃ samāśrayet |**
Yugapac ca dvayaṃ tyaktvā madhye tattvaṃ prakāśate | |
When one has knowledge or perception of any two thoughts, one should simultaneously leave both aside, and reside in the center between the two. In the center, one's true nature shines forth.

62) **Bhāve tyakte niruddhā cin naiva bhāvantaraṃ vrajet |**
Tadā tanmadhyabhāvena vikasatyati bhāvanā | |
When the mind has left a thought, and is restrained from moving towards another thought, it comes to rest in the

middle. Then, through that middle state of being, one's true nature blossoms brilliantly.

63) **Sarvaṃ dehaṃ cinmayaṃ hi jagad vā paribhāvayet |**
Yugapan nirvikalpena manasā paramodayaḥ | |
With mind free of thoughts, consider firmly one's entire body or the entire universe, to be consciousness. Then – the Supreme Awakening.

64) **Vāyudvayasya saṃghaṭṭād antarvā bahir antataḥ |**
Yogī samatvavijñānasamudgamanabhājanam | |
Concentrate on either of the two meeting points of one's breath – internal or external. The yogi will experience the birth of perfect understanding.

65) **Sarvaṃ jagat svadehaṃ vā svānandabharitaṃ smaret |**
Yugapat svāmṛtenaiva parānandamayo bhavet | |
One should consider one's entire body or the entire universe to be full of one's own bliss. Then, through one's own nectar of bliss, one will be full of the Supreme Bliss.

66) **Kuhanena prayogeṇa sadya eva mṛgekṣaṇe |**
Samudeti mahānando yena tattvaṃ prakāśate | |
O Deer Eyed One, great joy arises instantly, while being caressed. Through that joy, one's true nature is manifested.

67) **Sarvasrotonibandhena prāṇaśaktyordhvayā śanaiḥ |**
Pipīlasparśavelāyāṃ prathate paramaṃ sukham | |
By closing all the senses, the Energy of Life rises up gradually through the center of the spine, and one feels

a tingling sensation like that of an ant moving on one. Utmost joy then spreads all over.

68) **Vahner viṣasya madhye tu cittaṃ sukhamayaṃ kṣipet |**
Kevalaṃ vāyupūrṇaṃ vā smarānandena yujyate | |
One should cast one's attention on the joy experienced, between the beginning and end of the sexual act. One will be completely filled with Energy, and through the bliss of love, one is united with God.

69) **Śaktisaṅgamasaṃkṣubdhaśaktyāveśāvasānikam |**
Yat sukhaṃ brahmatattvasya tat sukhaṃ svākyam ucyate | |
At the time of sexual intercourse with a woman, there is great joy during an orgasm. That joy speaks of God's nature, and is of one's own self.

70) **Lehanāmanthanākoṭaiḥ strīsukhasya bharāt smṛteḥ |**
Śaktyabhāve 'pi deveśi bhaved ānandasaṃplavaḥ | |
O Goddess, even in the absence of a woman – from the memory of the intense joy of the climax, while making love to a woman – one will experience a flood of joy.

71) **Ānande mahati prāpte dṛṣṭe vā bāndhave cirāt |**
Ānandam udgataṃ dhyātvā tallayas tanmanā bhavet | |
Whenever great joy is obtained, or when joy arises on seeing a friend or relative after a long time, one should meditate on that joy. Then the mind will be absorbed into joy.

72) **Jagdhipānakṛtollāsarasānandavijṛmbhaṇāt |**
Bhāvayed bharitāvasthām mahānandas tato bhavet | |
From the pleasure of eating and drinking, one experiences joy blossoming. One should become filled with that state of joy. Then great joy will be obtained.

73) **Gītādiviṣayāsvādāsamasaukhyaikatātmanaḥ |**
Yoginas tanmayatvena manorūḍhes tadātmatā | |
When one is enjoying singing and other pleasures of the senses, great joy arises. The yogi should become one with that joy. Then, one experiences growth of self.

74) **Yatra yatra manas tuṣṭir manas tatraiva dhārayet |**
Tatra tatra parānandasvarūpaṃ sampravartate | |
Wherever the mind finds satisfaction – in that very place focus one's attention. Then, the Supreme Bliss of one's true nature will manifest itself.

75) **Anāgatāyāṃ nidrāyām praṇaṣṭe bāhyagocare |**
Sāvasthā manasā gamyā parā devī prakāśate | |
Concentrate on the state where sleep has not fully appeared, but the external world has disappeared. In that state, the Supreme Goddess is revealed.

76) **Tejasā sūryadīpāderākāśe śabalīkṛte |**
Dṛṣṭir niveśyā tatraiva svātmarūpam prakāśate | |
One should fix one's sight on the place where light from the sun, lamp, etc. forms different colors. There indeed, one's True Self will reveal itself.

77) **Karaṅkiṇyā krodhanayā bhairavyā lelihānayā |**
Khecaryā dṛṣṭikāle ca parāvāptiḥ prakāśate | |
From the yogic practices of Karankini, Krodhana, Bhairavi, Lelihana and Khecari Mudras, the Supreme Reality is revealed.

78) **Mṛdvāsane sphijaikena hastapādau nirāśrayam |**
Nidhāya tatprasaṅgena parā pūrṇā matirbhavet | |
Sit by placing one buttock on a soft seat, with no support for the hands and feet. By staying in that position, one will be filled with the understanding of the Supreme Reality.

79) **Upaviśyāsane samyak bāhū kṛtvārdhakuñcitau |**
Kakṣavyomni manaḥ kurvan śamam āyāti tallayāt | |
Sitting comfortably, curve the arms overhead, in the form of an arch. By absorbing the mind in the space of the armpits, Great Peace will come.

80) **Sthūlarūpasya bhāvasya stabdhāṃ dṛṣṭiṃ nipātya ca |**
Acireṇa nirādhāram manaḥ kṛtvā śivaṃ vrajet | |
Look firmly without blinking, at the gross form of any object. The mind will be without support, and within a short while one will reside in Shiva.

81) **Madhyajihve sphāritāsye madhye nikṣipya cetanām |**
Hoccāram manasā kurvaṃs tataḥ śānte pralīyate | |
With mouth wide open, throw the tongue upwards to the center of the palate. Fix attention on the middle of

the tongue, and feel the sound Ha being uttered there. Then, one will be dissolved in Peace.

82) **Āsane śayane sthitvā nirādhāraṃ vibhāvayan |**
Svadeham, manasi kṣīṇe, kṣaṇāt kṣīṇāśayo bhavet | |
Seated on a bed or couch, continuously imagine one's own body to be without support. The instant the mind disappears, one's fixed place of residence disappears.

83) **Calāsane sthitasyātha śanair vā dehacālanāt |**
Praśānte mānase bhāve devi divyaughamāpnuyāt | |
O Goddess, by experiencing the rhythmic movement of the body in a moving vehicle, or in a still place by swinging the body slowly. Then the mind becomes calm, and one obtains a flood of divinity.

84) **Ākāśaṃ vimalaṃ paśyan kṛtvā dṛṣṭiṃ nirantarām |**
Stabdhātmā tatkṣaṇād devi bhairavaṃ vapur āpnuyāt | |
Look continuously at a clear sky, without moving oneself. From that moment O Goddess, one will obtain the form of God.

85) **Līnaṃ mūrdhni viyat sarvaṃ bhairavatvena bhāvayet |**
Tat sarvaṃ bhairavākāratejastattvaṃ samāviśet | |
One should meditate that the entire space or sky, is absorbed in one's head. By absorbing the qualities of God, one will acquire the brilliant form of God.

86) **Kiṃcij jñātaṃ dvaitadāyi bāhyālokas tamaḥ punaḥ |**
Viśvādi bhairavaṃ rūpaṃ jñātvānantaprakāśabhṛt | |
In the waking state there is some knowledge born of duality. In the dream state there are impressions of the exterior. In deep sleep there is complete darkness. Know all these states of consciousness to be the form of God. Then, one will be filled with the infinite light of God.

87) **Evam eva durniśāyāṃ kṛṣṇapakṣāgame ciram |**
Taimiraṃ bhāvayan rūpaṃ bhairavaṃ rūpam eṣyati | |
Similarly, on a completely dark night during the dark half of the lunar month, concentrate for a long time on the darkness. One will then be propelled towards the form of God.

88) **Evam eva nimīlyādau netre kṛṣṇābham agrataḥ |**
Prasārya bhairavaṃ rūpaṃ bhāvayaṃs tanmayo bhavet | |
Similarly, in the absence of a dark night, close the eyes and concentrate on the darkness in front of one. Opening the eyes, see the dark form of God spreading everywhere. One will then become one with God.

89) **Yasya kasyendriyasyāpi vyāghātāc ca nirodhataḥ |**
Praviṣṭasyādvaye śūnye tatraivātmā prakāśate | |
When any sense organ is obstructed externally or is restrained by one, from carrying out its function – one will then enter the void that is beyond duality. There indeed, one's True Self will be revealed.

90) **Abindum avisargaṃ ca akāraṃ japato mahān |**
Udeti devi sahasā jñānaughaḥ parameśvaraḥ | |
Continuously recite the vowel A, without the sound M or H. Then O Goddess, a great flood of knowledge of God rises forcefully.

91) **Varṇasya savisargasya visargāntaṃ citiṃ kuru |**
Nirādhāreṇa cittena spṛśed brahma sanātanam | |
Make the sound H and concentrate on the end of the sound. As the mind will be without support, one will permanently touch God.

92) **Vyomākāraṃ svam ātmānaṃ dhyāyed digbhir anāvṛtam |**
Nirāśrayā citiḥ śaktiḥ svarūpaṃ darśayet tadā | |
Meditate on one's own self in the form of space (or the sky), unlimited in all directions. Then, one will see one's own form as the unsupported energy of consciousness.

93) **Kiñcid aṅgaṃ vibhidyādau tīkṣṇasūcyādinā tataḥ |**
Tatraiva cetanāṃ yuktvā bhairave nirmalā gatiḥ | |
Pierce any part of your body with a sharp needle, point, etc. Then join your awareness to that very place. There, you will obtain the purity of God.

94) **Cittādyantaḥkṛtir nāsti mamāntar bhāvayed iti |**
Vikalpānām abhāvena vikalpair ujjhito bhavet | |
One should meditate like this – "There is nothing inside me. No mind, intellect, bones, organs, etc." By this

meditation one will abandon all thoughts. By being in a state without thoughts, one will reach God.

95) **Māyā vimohinī nāma kalāyāḥ kalanaṃ sthitam |**
Ityādidharmaṃ tattvānāṃ kalayan na pṛthag bhavet | |
Remain firm in one's understanding that a small part of anything, with a name, is a tempting illusion. Thus, the primary quality of one's true nature is unity. From this understanding one will not remain separate any longer.

96) **Jhagitīcchāṃ samutpannām avalokya śamaṃ nayet |**
Yata eva samudbhūtā tatas tatraiva līyate | |
When one sees a desire having risen, one should immediately end it. One will then be absorbed in the very place from which the desire arose.

97) **Yadā mamecchā notpannā jñānaṃ vā, kas tadāsmi vai |**
Tattvato 'haṃ tathābhūtas tallīnas tanmanā bhavet | |
When desire or knowledge have not arisen in me – who am I?, in that condition. That is truly my essential Reality. By reflecting in this way, one will be absorbed into that Reality.

98) **Ichhāyām athavā jñāne jāte cittaṃ niveśayet |**
Ātmabuddhyānanyacetās tatas tattvārthadarśanam | |
When desire or knowledge have arisen, one should stop reflecting on them, and consider the Self as identical with consciousness. Then, one's true nature appears.

99) **Nirnimittaṃ bhavej jñānaṃ nirādhāraṃ bhramātmakam |**
Tattvataḥ kasyacin naitad evaṃbhāvī śivaḥ priye | |

The true nature of God is without cause and without support. Any person's knowledge or perception is not this. O Dear One, in this way, one becomes Shiva.

100) **Ciddharmā sarvadeheṣu viśeṣo nāsti kutracit |**
Ataśca tanmayaṃ sarvaṃ bhāvayan bhavajij janaḥ ||
Consciousness is the essential quality in all bodies. There is no difference anywhere. Therefore, everything is made of the same consciousness. By understanding this, a person is victorious over worldly existence.

101) **Kāmakrodhalobhamohamadamātsaryagocare |**
Buddhiṃ nistimitāṃ kṛtvā tat tattvam avaśiṣyate ||
When strong emotions of desire, anger, greed, infatuation, intoxication or jealousy appear – stop the mind! By doing that, the True Reality underlying those emotions, appears.

102) **Indrajālamayaṃ viśvaṃ vyastaṃ vā citrakarmavat |**
Bhramad vā dhyāyataḥ sarvaṃ paśyataśca sukhodgamaḥ ||
See the whole world and all its separate moving objects, as a magic show, or an illusion, or like a picture. From this meditation, joy arises.

103) **Na cittaṃ nikṣiped duḥkhe na sukhe vā parikṣipet |**
Bhairavi jñāyatāṃ madhye kiṃ tattvam avaśiṣyate ||
One should not place their thoughts on pleasure or pain. O Goddess, know that True Reality lies between the two.

104) **Vihāya nijadehāsthāṃ sarvatrāsmīti bhāvayan |**
Dṛḍhena manasā dṛṣṭyā nānyekṣiṇyā sukhī bhavet | |
Leave behind concern for one's body. With a firm mind and vision for nothing else, believe – "I am everywhere." Then, one will attain joy.

105) **Ghaṭādau yac ca vijñānam icchādyaṃ vā, mamāntare |**
Naiva sarvagataṃ jātaṃ bhāvayann iti sarvagaḥ | |
"Knowledge, desire, etc. exist not only within me, but everywhere in jars, and other objects." With this belief, one becomes omnipresent.

106) **Grāhyagrāhakasaṃvittiḥ sāmānyā sarvadehinām |**
Yogināṃ tu viśeṣo 'sti saṃbandhe sāvadhānatā | |
The awareness of object and subject is common to all living beings. However, the yogis have the distinction that they are always aware of the self.

107) **Svavad anyaśarīre 'pi saṃvittim anubhāvayet |**
Apekṣāṃ svaśarīrasya tyaktvā vyāpī dinair bhavet | |
Leaving aside concern for one's own body, one should continuously believe that the same consciousness is present in oneself and also in other bodies. In a few days, one will be all pervading.

108) **Nirādhāraṃ manaḥ kṛtvā vikalpān na vikalpayet |**
Tadātmaparamātmatve bhairavo mṛgalocane | |
O Deer Eyed One, by stopping all thoughts, the mind

will be without support. Then the self will become the Supreme Self of God.

109) **Sarvajñaḥ sarvakartā ca vyāpakaḥ parameśvaraḥ |**
Sa evāhaṃ śaivadharmā iti dārḍhyād bhavec chivaḥ | |
God is omniscient, omnipotent and omnipresent. Believe firmly, "I have those same qualities of God." Then, one becomes God.

110) **Jalasyevormayo vahner jvālābhaṅgyaḥ prabhā raveḥ |**
Mamaiva bhairavasyaitā viśvabhaṅgyo vibheditāḥ | |
Just as waves arise from water, flames from fire, light from the sun – in the same way, the various forms of the universe have arisen from Me, God.

111) **Bhrāntvā bhrāntvā śarīreṇa tvaritaṃ bhuvi pātanāt |**
Kṣobhaśaktivirāmeṇa parā saṃjāyate daśā | |
One should swiftly turn his body round and round, till he falls to the ground. At the end of the energy of motion, the Supreme State is born.

112) **Ādhāreṣv athavā 'śaktyā 'jñānāccittalayena vā |**
Jātaśaktisamāveśakṣobhānte bhairavaṃ vapuḥ | |
When there is lack of energy or lack of knowledge, the mind is dissolved, and one is absorbed into energy. In the end, when the energy subsides, God appears.

113) **Saṃpradāyam imaṃ devi śṛṇu samyag vadāmyaham |**
Kaivalyaṃ jāyate sadyo netrayoḥ stabdhamātrayoḥ | |

O Goddess, listen carefully, as I explain the mystic tradition. If one's eyes are fixed without blinking, unification with the Supreme, will occur immediately.

114) **Saṃkocaṃ karṇayoḥ kṛtvā hy adhodvāre tathaiva ca |**
Anackam ahalaṃ dhyāyan viśed brahma sanātanam | |
Close the ears, and compress the opening of the rectum. Then by meditating on the sound without vowel or consonant, one permanently enters God.

115) **Kūpādike mahāgarte sthitvopari nirīkṣaṇāt |**
Avikalpamateḥ samyak sadyaś cittalayaḥ sphuṭam | |
Stand over a deep well, etc. and look without blinking at the deep hollow space. The mind becomes completely free of thoughts, and then the mind is immediately dissolved.

116) **Yatra yatra mano yāti bāhye vābhyantare 'pi vā |**
Tatra tatra śivāvasthā vyāpakatvāt kva yāsyati | |
Wherever the mind goes, externally or internally, everywhere there is the form of Shiva. As God is omnipresent, where will the mind go?

117) **Yatra yatrākṣamārgeṇa caitanyaṃ vyajyate vibhoḥ |**
Tasya tanmātradharmitvāc cillayād bharitātmatā | |
Whenever awareness is increased through any sense organ, remain in that awareness. Then, the mind will be dissolved and one will be filled with the Supreme Self.

118) **Kṣutādyante bhaye śoke gahvare vā raṇād drute |**
Kutūhale kṣudhādyante brahmasattāmayī daśā | |
At the commencement and end of a sneeze, during danger, sorrow, weeping, flight from a battlefield, during curiosity, at the commencement and end of hunger. These states are full of the State of God.

119) **Vastuṣu smaryamāṇeṣu dṛṣṭe deśe manas tyajet |**
Svaśarīraṃ nirādhāraṃ kṛtvā prasarati prabhuḥ | |
Leaving concern for one's body, remember the sight of a place, object or incident. The mind will be without support and one experiences a flood of Divinity.

120) **Kvacid vastuni vinyasya śanair dṛṣṭiṃ nivartayet |**
Taj jñānaṃ cittasahitaṃ devi śūnyālayo bhavet | |
After looking at some object, one should slowly withdraw their sight from it, then their knowledge together with their thought of it. O Goddess, one will then reside in the Void.

121) **Bhaktyudrekād viraktasya yādṛśī jāyate matiḥ |**
Sā śaktiḥ śāṅkarī nityaṃ bhāvayet tāṃ tataḥ śivaḥ | |
From an abundance of devotion and a detached nature, an understanding of Shiva's Energy is born. One should continuously be her. Then, Shiva.

122) **Vastvantare vedyamāne sarvavastuṣu śūnyatā |**
Tām eva manasā dhyātvā vidito 'pi praśāmyati | |

Understand an object is empty inside. Emptiness is also a feature of all objects. With mind free of thoughts, meditate on that emptiness. Then, even though the object is perceived or known, one becomes calm.

123) **Kiṃcijjñair yā smṛtā śuddhiḥ sā śuddhiḥ śambhudarśane |**
Na śucir hy aśucis tasmān-nirvikalpaḥ sukhī bhavet | |
That considered to be pure by people of little understanding, is neither pure nor impure in the Shaiva system of philosophy. One who rises above dualizing thoughts attains complete happiness.

124) **Sarvatra bhairavo bhāvaḥ sāmānyeṣv api gocaraḥ |**
Na ca tadvyatirekeṇa paro 'stīty advayā gatiḥ | |
"God is existing everywhere, common in all. There is nothing else other than God." With this knowledge, one attains the non-dual condition.

125) **Samaḥ śatrau ca mitre ca samo mānāvamānayoḥ |**
Brahmaṇaḥ paripūrṇatvād iti jñātvā sukhī bhavet | |
From knowing that God completely fills everything, one is the same towards enemy and friend, in honor and dishonor. With this attitude, one obtains joy.

126) **Na dveṣaṃ bhāvayet kvāpi na rāgaṃ bhāvayet kvacit |**
Rāgadveṣavinirmuktau madhye brahma prasarpati | |
There should be no feeling of aversion or attraction towards any person or place. By remaining in the center between the two, one is liberated from the duality of

aversion and attraction. Then, one experiences God spreading everywhere.

127) **Yad avedyaṃ yad agrāhyaṃ yac chūnyaṃ yad abhāvagam |**
Tat sarvaṃ bhairavaṃ bhāvyaṃ tadante bodhasaṃbhavaḥ | |
That which is beyond knowledge, beyond grasping, beyond not being, that which is void – contemplate all that to be God. In the end, the birth of enlightenment.

128) **Nitye nirāśraye śūnye vyāpake kalanojjhite |**
Bāhyākāśe manaḥ kṛtvā nirākāśaṃ samāviśet | |
Fix the mind on external space, which is eternal, supportless, void, all pervasive and silent. By doing this, one will completely enter non-space.

129) **Yatra yatra mano yāti tattat tenaiva tatkṣaṇam |**
Parityajyānavasthityā nistaraṅgas tato bhavet | |
Wherever the mind goes, at that very moment, one should leave that thought. By not allowing the mind to settle into thoughts, one will be free of thoughts.

130) **Bhayā sarvaṃ ravayati sarvado vyāpako 'khile |**
Iti bhairavaśabdasya santatoccāraṇāc chivaḥ | |
God gives rise to everything, pervades everything and every sound. Therefore, by continuously reciting the word Bhairava , one becomes Shiva.

131) **Ahaṃ mamedam ityādi pratipattiprasaṅgataḥ |**
Nirādhāre mano yāti taddhyānapreraṇāc chamī | |

"I am, this is mine, etc." On the occasion of this assertion, let the mind go to that which is without support. From the impelling force of this meditation, one attains Peace.

132) **Nityo vibhur nirādhāro vyāpakaś cākhilādhipaḥ |**
Śabdān pratikṣaṇaṃ dhyāyan kṛtārtho 'rthānurūpataḥ ||
"Eternal, omnipresent, supportless, all pervasive and Lord of the Entire Universe." By meditating every moment on these words, in conformity with one's object, one obtains one's object.

133) **Atattvam indrajālābham idaṃ sarvam avasthitam |**
Kiṃ tattvam indrajālasya iti dārḍhyāc chamaṃ vrajet ||
The entire universe is not real. It's appearance is an illusion. "What is real about an illusion?" From believing this firmly, one abides in Peace.

134) **Ātmano nirvikārasya kva jñānaṃ kva ca vā kriyā |**
Jñānāyattā bahirbhāvā ataḥ śūnyam idaṃ jagat ||
The Self is unchangeable. Where is there knowledge or activity? External existence or objects are dependent of knowledge. Therefore this world is void.

135) **Na me bandho na mokṣo me bhītasyaitā vibhīṣikāḥ |**
Pratibimbam idaṃ buddher jaleṣv iva vivasvataḥ ||
Neither bondage nor liberation for me. Those terrified of these concepts should see them as images of the mind, just like the image of the sun in water.

136) **Indriyadvārakaṃ sarvaṃ sukhaduḥkhādisaṅgamam |**
Itīndriyāṇi saṃtyajya svasthaḥ svātmani vartate ||
All contact with pleasure, pain, etc., are through the sense organs. Therefore, one should detach oneself from the senses, turn within and abide in one's own self.

137) **Jñānaprakāśakaṃ sarvaṃ sarveṇātmā prakāśakaḥ |**
Ekam ekasvabhāvatvāt jñānaṃ jñeyaṃ vibhāvyate ||
All things are revealed by the knower. The Self is revealed through all things. As their own nature is the same, perceive the knower and the known as one.

138) **Mānasaṃ cetanā śaktir ātmā ceti catuṣṭayam |**
Yadā priye parikṣīṇaṃ tadā tad bhairavaṃ vapuḥ ||
Mind, intellect, energy of life and limited self. O Dear One, when this group of four disappears, then the state of God appears.

139) **Nistaraṅgopadeśānāṃ śatam uktaṃ samāsataḥ |**
Dvādaśābhyadhikaṃ devi yajjñātvā jñānavij janaḥ ||
O Goddess, I have described in brief a hundred and twelve meditations, by which a person can still the mind. Knowing them, a person becomes wise.

140) **Atra caikatame yukto jāyate bhairavaḥ svayam |**
Vācā karoti karmāṇi śāpānugrahakārakaḥ ||
By being proficient in any one of these practices, a person will be united with God, and God will be born within oneself. One can then perform any work with his word

alone. One will have the ability to confer malediction or benediction.

141) **Ajarāmaratām eti so 'ṇimādiguṇānvitaḥ |**
Yoginīnāṃ priyo devi sarvamelāpakādhipaḥ ||
Jīvann api vimukto 'sau kurvannapi na lipyate |
He becomes immortal and free from old age. He is endowed with the power of becoming as small as an atom, and with other powers. O Goddess, he becomes the favorite of the female yogis, and the master of spiritual gatherings. Even while living, he is liberated. Though he performs worldly activities, he is not affected by them.

Śrī Devī uvāca
The Goddess said:

142) **Idaṃ yadi vapur deva parāyāś ca maheśvara ||**
O God, if this is the nature of the Supreme Energy,

143) **Evamuktavyavasthāyāṃ japyate ko japaś ca kaḥ |**
Dhyāyate ko mahānātha pūjyate kaś ca tṛpyati ||
Hūyate kasya vā homo yāgaḥ kasya ca kiṃ katham |
as described, then who will one continuously recite a mantra on, and what will one recite? O Great Lord, who is to be meditated on, who is be worshipped, and who is to be gratified? To whom does one offer oblations to or perform sacrifices for, and in what way?

Śrī Bhairava uvāca

God said:

144) **Eṣātra prakriyā bāhyā sthūleṣv eva mṛgekṣaṇe | |**
O Deer Eyed One, these practices referred to are external and only pertain to gross forms.

145) **Bhūyo bhūyaḥ pare bhāve bhāvanā bhāvyate hi yā |**
Japaḥ so 'tra svayaṃ nādo mantrātmā japya īdṛśaḥ | |
That meditation made again and again on the Supreme Being is continuous mantra recitation. One should meditate on the spontaneous sound that continues within oneself in the form of a mantra. This is what mantra chanting is really about.

146) **Dhyānaṃ hi niścalā buddhir nirākārā nirāśrayā |**
Na tu dhyānaṃ śarīrākṣimukhahastādikalpanā | |
Meditation is unswerving concentration without form or support. Concentration on an imaginary figure of the Divine with body, eyes, face, hands, etc., is not meditation.

147) **Pūjā nāma na puṣpādyair yā matiḥ kriyate dṛḍhā |**
Nirvikalpe mahāvyomni sā pūjā hy ādarāl layaḥ | |
Offering of flowers, etc., is not called worship. One should firmly fix the heart on the Supreme Space, which is beyond thought. From that love, there is union with God. That indeed is worship.

148) **Atraikatamayuktisthe yotpadyeta dinād dinam |**
Bharitākāratā sātra tṛptir atyantapūrṇatā | |
By being established in even one of the meditations explained here, one will experience consciousness rising day after day, till one reaches the Highest State. That is known here as satisfaction.

149) **Mahāśūnyālaye vahnau bhūtākṣaviṣayādikam |**
Hūyate manasā sārdhaṃ sa homaś cetanā-srucā | |
When the organs of sense, objects of sense, etc., are offered along with the mind, to be dissolved in the fire of the Supreme Void, with consciousness as a ladle – that is real oblation.

150) **Yāgo 'tra parameśāni tuṣṭir ānandalakṣaṇā |**
Kṣapaṇāt sarvapāpānāṃ trāṇāt sarvasya pārvati | |
O Parvati, from destroying all of one's sins, one is completely absorbed into the Supreme Being, and obtains satisfaction described as bliss. This is the meaning of sacrifice in this system.

151) **Rudraśaktisamāveśas tat kṣetraṃ bhāvanā parā |**
Anyathā tasya tattvasya kā pūjā kaś ca tṛpyati | |
The union of God and Energy. That Supreme State should be one's place of pilgrimage. Otherwise, in one's true state, who will worship and who will one satisfy?

152) **Svatantrānandacinmātrasāraḥ svātmā hi sarvataḥ |**
Āveśanaṃ tatsvarūpe svātmanaḥ snānam īritam | |

The essence of one's Self consists entirely of freedom, bliss and consciousness. Immersing our limited self into our True Self, is bathing.

153) **Yair eva pūjyate dravyais tarpyate vā parāparaḥ |**
Yaś caiva pūjakaḥ sarvaḥ sa evaikaḥ kva pūjanam | |
The objects with which worship is to be done, or with which the Higher and Lower Reality is to be satisfied, the worshipper, and God are in fact all one and the same. Why then, this worship?

154) **Vrajet prāṇo viśej jīva icchayā kuṭilākṛtiḥ |**
Dīrghātmā sā mahādevī parakṣetraṃ parāparā | |
The breath goes out and the breath comes in spontaneously, in a curved manner. She reaches far, higher and lower. The Great Goddess is the supreme place of pilgrimage.

155) **Asyām anucaran tiṣṭhan mahānandamaye 'dhvare |**
Tayā devyā samāviṣṭaḥ paraṃ bhairavam āpnuyāt | |
This fire (Goddess) is full of Great Bliss. By following her and resting in her, one becomes fully identified with her. Then, through the Goddess, one obtains God.

a) **Sakāreṇa bahir yāti hakāreṇa viśet punaḥ |**
Haṃsahaṃsety amuṃ mantraṃ jīvo japati nityaśaḥ | |
The breath makes the sound Sa when it goes outside, and again makes the sound Ha when it enters inside. "Hamsa, Hamsa." This mantra is continuously recited by a living being,

156) **Sakāreṇa bahir yāti hakāreṇa viśet punaḥ |**
Haṃsahaṃsety amuṃ mantraṃ jīvo japati nityaśaḥ | |
21,600 times during a day and night. This continuous recitation of the Goddess fully described, is easy to attain. It is difficult only for the senseless.

157) **Ityetat kathitaṃ devi paramāmṛtam uttamam |**
Etac ca naiva kasyāpi prakāśyaṃ tu kadācana | |
O Goddess, with these words, I have explained the supreme teaching, which leads one to the highest state of immortality. This teaching should not be revealed to just anyone.

158) **Paraśiṣye khale krūre abhakte gurupādayoḥ |**
Nirvikalpamatīnāṃ tu vīrāṇām unnatātmanām | |
Particularly to pupils of another tradition, or pupils who are wicked, cruel, and unfaithful to their master. On the contrary, it may be fearlessly given to the brave ones, whose minds are free of doubts,

159) **Bhaktānāṃ guruvargasya dātavyaṃ nirviśaṅkayā |**
Grāmo rājyaṃ puraṃ deśaḥ putradārakuṭumbakam | |
and who are devoted to their line of masters. One's race, government, city, country, children, wife and family –

160) **Sarvam etat parityajya grāhyam etan mṛgekṣaṇe |**
Kim ebhir asthirair devi sthiraṃ param idaṃ dhanam | |
One should give all this up, O Deer Eyed One. What is the point in these temporary things? Instead, O

Goddess, one should seize this teaching, which leads to the everlasting, supreme treasure.

161) **Prāṇā api pradātavyā na deyaṃ paramāmṛtam |**
Life may even be renounced, but this teaching which leads to the supreme nectar of immortality, should not be given to undeserving ones.

Śrī Devī uvāca
The Goddess said:

Devadeva mahādeva paritṛptāsmi śaṅkara | |
O God, O God of Gods, O Great God, I am completely satisfied.

162) **Rudrayāmalatantrasya sāram adyāvadhāritam |**
Sarvaśaktiprabhedānāṃ hṛdayaṃ jñātam adya ca | |
I have now fully understood the essence of the Rudrayamala Tantra, and the essence of the different grades of Energy.

163) **Ity uktvānanditā devī kaṇṭhe lagnā śivasya tu | |**
Having said these words, the Goddess who was filled with joy, then embraced God.